Distinguished Wisdom Presents . . .
"GAIN 20/20 VISION FOR THE NEW DECADE"
2022 – 365 DAY JOURNAL

Document Your Journey!

Pastor Terrance Levise Turner, MBA

Well Spoken Inc. | *Nashville, TN.*

© 2021 Terrance Levise Turner
All rights reserved. No part of this publication may be reproduced, scanned, transmitted or distributed in any printed or electronic or mechanical forms or methods, including photocopying, recording, or other without prior written permission of the publisher, except in the case of brief select quotations embodied in critical reviews and certain other noncommercial uses permitted by copyright law. For permission requests, write to the publisher, addressed below.

Unless otherwise indicated, all Scripture quotations are taken from the King James Version of the Bible.

Well Spoken Inc.
P.O. Box 291806 Nashville, TN. 37229
WellSpokenInc@bellsouth.net
www.TerranceTurnerLivingProverbs.com

Ordering Information
Quantity sales. Special discounts are available on quantity purchases by corporations, associations, and others. For details, contact the "Special Sales Department" at the address above.

Cover design by Susan of LSDdesign/99Designs.com
Book design by Terrance Levise Turner
Printed in the United States of America
ISBN 9781734482072 Paperback

Introduction

The Benefits of Journaling

Journaling has so many benefits for you, such as reducing anxiety in today's circumstances and uncertainty in society. God can give you answers as you take time to meditate upon His Word and let Him bring clarity to your mind. This journal gives you the opportunity to capture your thoughts and ideas as you pursue your goals. Journaling gives you hope for the future as you consider the good things that God does for you everyday. Journaling allows you to develop a "thankfulness record." You can keep track of the various blessings and goodness that God shows you, big and small. This will bring more joy in your life and help you to have a grateful and more peaceful perspective. Journaling also allows you to discover a brighter perspective regarding areas of your life that you may not have thought of before. As you read the book **Gain 20/20 Vision For The New Decade! A Step By Step For A More Successful Future!** you will discover principles you will want to take notes on how to apply. You will also want to reflect further on your goals that you write down in the **Gain 20/20 Vision For The New Decade! 10-Year Calendar 2020-2030: A Decade of Achievement!** You will want to further document your discoveries over the next decade on how planning and goal-setting changes your life. Please enjoy writing in this journal for the entire year. You will create a valuable record of your treasured thoughts. You will be so glad that you decided to "Document Your Journey!"

Gain 20/20 Vision For The New Decade!
2022 – 365 Day Journal
Document Your Journey!

Living Proverb #1603: "If you can see farther than where you came from, then, you can go further and be more than where you came from."

~~**Pastor Terrance Levise Turner, MBA**

Gain 20/20 Vision For The New Decade!
2022 – 365 Day Journal
Document Your Journey!

Living Proverb #1601: "In once-in-a-lifetime opportunities, you have to use your *"mind-biscuit"* to *sop-up* all of the gravy off of the plate. Tomorrow is not promised."

~~Pastor Terrance Levise Turner, MBA

Gain 20/20 Vision For The New Decade!
2022 – 365 Day Journal
Document Your Journey!

Living Proverb #1604: "Harvest season always comes. It may not come as fast as you want it to come, but the more that you truly want it to come, the faster it will come."

~~**Pastor Terrance Levise Turner, MBA**

Gain 20/20 Vision For The New Decade!
2022 – 365 Day Journal
Document Your Journey!

Living Proverb #1605: "Keep on serving God, and stay on the *blessing* side of the Word."

~~Pastor Terrance Levise Turner, MBA

Gain 20/20 Vision For The New Decade!
2022 – 365 Day Journal
Document Your Journey!

Living Proverb #1606: "If you honor Jesus, and His principles, you will do well. It's not just about loving Jesus. Rather, to be successful, you have to obey the principles of His Word."

~~**Pastor Terrance Levise Turner, MBA**

Gain 20/20 Vision For The New Decade!
2022 – 365 Day Journal
Document Your Journey!

Living Proverb #1608: "To make your money independent of being dependent is better."

~~Pastor Terrance Levise Turner, MBA

Gain 20/20 Vision For The New Decade!
2022 – 365 Day Journal
Document Your Journey!

Living Proverb #1609: "When your blessing comes, it's a matter of fulfillment of a promise, and not a matter of a miracle. It's simply because you obeyed God's principles"

~~**Pastor Terrance Levise Turner, MBA**

Gain 20/20 Vision For The New Decade!
2022 – 365 Day Journal
Document Your Journey!

Living Proverb #1610: "God is not new at causing people to succeed. What He has done for others, He will do for you. All you have to do is obey His principles of faith, wisdom, and diligence."

~~**Pastor Terrance Levise Turner, MBA**

Gain 20/20 Vision For The New Decade!
2022 – 365 Day Journal
Document Your Journey!

Living Proverb #1611: "Whatever may be your sorrow, pain, failure, or disappointment, know that God is your source of redemption, joy, and lifelong victory."

~~**Pastor Terrance Levise Turner, MBA**

Gain 20/20 Vision For The New Decade!
2022 – 365 Day Journal
Document Your Journey!

Living Proverb #1613: "If God be for you, who can be against you? If God be for you, who else really matters? If God be for you, He can subdue your adversaries."

~~**Pastor Terrance Levise Turner, MBA**

Gain 20/20 Vision For The New Decade!
2022 – 365 Day Journal
Document Your Journey!

Living Proverb #1614: "*Be* who you are, and people will see who you are, and you won't have to *say* who you are. You don't have to brag. Let your *works* speak louder than your words."

~~**Pastor Terrance Levise Turner, MBA**

Gain 20/20 Vision For The New Decade!
2022 – 365 Day Journal
Document Your Journey!

Living Proverb #1617: *"In relationships, sometimes it's not your words that are needed. It's your listening ear. Often, just through your time and understanding, people can untangle themselves."*

~~**Pastor Terrance Levise Turner, MBA**

Gain 20/20 Vision For The New Decade!
2022 – 365 Day Journal
Document Your Journey!

Living Proverb #1618a: *"Success is not a random miracle. Success is a sure process. If you follow success principles, you will succeed. Success is the norm, and not the exception."*
~~**Pastor Terrance Levise Turner, MBA**

Gain 20/20 Vision For The New Decade!
2022 – 365 Day Journal
Document Your Journey!

Living Proverb #1618b: *"If you follow the sure patterns that have been successfully traversed, recorded, and shared, you will succeed faster. Get wisdom. It's the principal thing for success."*

~~**Pastor Terrance Levise Turner, MBA**

Gain 20/20 Vision For The New Decade!
2022 – 365 Day Journal
Document Your Journey!

Living Proverb #1619: *"Allow the light of God to fully shine through you this week. Show your difference. Show your love. Show your brilliance. Shine for Jesus! You are the light of the world!"*

*~~***Pastor Terrance Levise Turner, MBA***

Gain 20/20 Vision For The New Decade!
2022 – 365 Day Journal
Document Your Journey!

Living Proverb #1620: *"You may have a lot of things to be concerned about, but pray. Jesus is in control. So, you have nothing to worry about."*

~~**Pastor Terrance Levise Turner, MBA**

Gain 20/20 Vision For The New Decade!
2022 – 365 Day Journal
Document Your Journey!

Living Proverb #1621: *"Often, the greatest friendship is correction."*

~~**Pastor Terrance Levise Turner, MBA**

Gain 20/20 Vision For The New Decade!
2022 – 365 Day Journal
Document Your Journey!

Living Proverb #1622: *"Truly great people are gracious people."*
~~Pastor Terrance Levise Turner, MBA

Gain 20/20 Vision For The New Decade!
2022 – 365 Day Journal
Document Your Journey!

Living Proverb #1623: *"There's rarely any drawback to being early. But, there's typically always a negative stigma to being late. Particularly, when you're cooperating with busy, diligent people."*

~~**Pastor Terrance Levise Turner, MBA**

Gain 20/20 Vision For The New Decade!
2022 – 365 Day Journal
Document Your Journey!

Living Proverb #1624: *"Some days you make happen. Some days make themselves happen. When you're led by the Holy Spirit your spirit can lead you faster than your mind can conceive."*

~~**Pastor Terrance Levise Turner, MBA**

Gain 20/20 Vision For The New Decade!
2022 – 365 Day Journal
Document Your Journey!

Living Proverb #1625: *"You don't need a sign. You need an assignment."*

~~**Pastor Terrance Levise Turner, MBA**

Gain 20/20 Vision For The New Decade!
2022 – 365 Day Journal
Document Your Journey!

Living Proverb #1626: *"Little people, with little opinions, make little difference. Keep your eyes on the prize. God knows your heart. He knows what you are accomplishing."*

~~**Pastor Terrance Levise Turner, MBA**

Gain 20/20 Vision For The New Decade!
2022 – 365 Day Journal
Document Your Journey!

Living Proverb #1629: *"Don't focus so much on waiting on your blessing to come toward you. Rather, focus on doing what's required so that you are moving toward your blessing."*

*~~***Pastor Terrance Levise Turner, MBA***

Gain 20/20 Vision For The New Decade!
2022 – 365 Day Journal
Document Your Journey!

Living Proverb #1630: *"The evident sign of genius is productivity."*

~~Pastor Terrance Levise Turner, MBA

Gain 20/20 Vision For The New Decade!
2022 – 365 Day Journal
Document Your Journey!

Living Proverb #1631: *"Success is a good investment. Once you get started, success is cumulative like compound interest."*
~~**Pastor Terrance Levise Turner, MBA**

Gain 20/20 Vision For The New Decade!
2022 – 365 Day Journal
Document Your Journey!

Living Proverb #1632: *"No matter what you're facing today, know that the Lord is working on your behalf! He loves you!"*
~~**Pastor Terrance Levise Turner, MBA**

Gain 20/20 Vision For The New Decade!
2022 – 365 Day Journal
Document Your Journey!

Living Proverb #1633: *"Praying without ceasing doesn't take a longtime. It just takes oftentimes."*

~~**Pastor Terrance Levise Turner, MBA**

Gain 20/20 Vision For The New Decade!
2022 – 365 Day Journal
Document Your Journey!

Living Proverb #1635: *"You're young enough for your dreams. You're strong enough for your dreams. You know enough to obtain your dreams. And you're well able to possess your land!"*

~~**Pastor Terrance Levise Turner, MBA**

Gain 20/20 Vision For The New Decade!
2022 – 365 Day Journal
Document Your Journey!

Living Proverb #1636: *"Anytime is a good time to take a praise break unto God for all of His goodness, mercy, and loving-kindness to you and your family! Praise Him! It will make you feel better!"*
~~**Pastor Terrance Levise Turner, MBA**

Gain 20/20 Vision For The New Decade!
2022 – 365 Day Journal
Document Your Journey!

Living Proverb #1637: *"No matter how you're helped by another person, always be aware of the tendency of human beings to want to control something. Whether it's a dog, a cat, or another person."*
~~**Pastor Terrance Levise Turner, MBA**

Gain 20/20 Vision For The New Decade!
2022 – 365 Day Journal
Document Your Journey!

Living Proverb #1637b: *"Always know your value, and demand mutual respect in relationships."*

~~Pastor Terrance Levise Turner, MBA

Gain 20/20 Vision For The New Decade!
2022 – 365 Day Journal
Document Your Journey!

Living Proverb #1638: *"Control yourself, and you won't be controlled by anyone else."*

~~Pastor Terrance Levise Turner, MBA

Gain 20/20 Vision For The New Decade!
2022 – 365 Day Journal
Document Your Journey!

Living Proverb #1646: *"Keep sowing good seed, because during harvest time, only the seed you've actually sown will come up."*
~~**Pastor Terrance Levise Turner, MBA**

Gain 20/20 Vision For The New Decade!
2022 – 365 Day Journal
Document Your Journey!

Living Proverb #1647: *"The greatest lesson that you can learn in life is the ability to think for yourself."*
~~**Pastor Terrance Levise Turner, MBA**

Gain 20/20 Vision For The New Decade!
2022 – 365 Day Journal
Document Your Journey!

Living Proverb #1649: *"In the game of life, if you want to play, you had better pray!"*

~~Pastor Terrance Levise Turner, MBA

Gain 20/20 Vision For The New Decade!
2022 – 365 Day Journal
Document Your Journey!

Living Proverb #1652: *"There's no better time to solve a problem than when it is a problem, so that it won't continue to be a problem."*

~~Pastor Terrance Levise Turner, MBA

Gain 20/20 Vision For The New Decade!
2022 – 365 Day Journal
Document Your Journey!

Living Proverb #1654: *"If you want to please God, just start moving in the direction. He knows your heart and He's not looking for perfection. Start taking steps, and God will get you there."*

~~**Pastor Terrance Levise Turner, MBA**

Gain 20/20 Vision For The New Decade!
2022 – 365 Day Journal
Document Your Journey!

Living Proverb #1655: *"If you respect money, money will respect you. If you disrespect money, money will leave you. Respecting money means to be watchful over it and it will stay with you."*
~~**Pastor Terrance Levise Turner, MBA**

Gain 20/20 Vision For The New Decade!
2022 – 365 Day Journal
Document Your Journey!

Living Proverb #1662: *"No matter what you may be facing today, no matter your circumstances, leave your care in the hand of the Lord, for He cares for you. He will make it alright."*

~~**Pastor Terrance Levise Turner, MBA**

Gain 20/20 Vision For The New Decade!
2022 – 365 Day Journal
Document Your Journey!

Living Proverb #1663: *"Wisdom is not knowledge. Knowledge must be pursued. Wise is the person who discerns that he or she needs more knowledge, and has the discipline to get it and use it."*

~~**Pastor Terrance Levise Turner, MBA**

Gain 20/20 Vision For The New Decade!
2022 – 365 Day Journal
Document Your Journey!

Living Proverb #1664: *"In financial decisions, the bottom line is the bottom line. If taking from your bottom line to give to someone else's bottom line causes your bottom line to grow, then do it."*

~~**Pastor Terrance Levise Turner, MBA**

Gain 20/20 Vision For The New Decade!
2022 – 365 Day Journal
Document Your Journey!

Living Proverb #1666: *"The future is in your hands. So, manage it well. What you do today will greatly impact tomorrow's outcomes."*
~~Pastor Terrance Levise Turner, MBA

Gain 20/20 Vision For The New Decade!
2022 – 365 Day Journal
Document Your Journey!

Living Proverb #1666: *"One speaker asked, 'Would you rather have 20 half carat diamonds, or one 10 carat diamond?' I say, 'I'll take both.' Everything has value when properly marketed."*

~~**Pastor Terrance Levise Turner, MBA**

Gain 20/20 Vision For The New Decade!
2022 – 365 Day Journal
Document Your Journey!

Living Proverb #1668: *"Marketing makes the revenue wheel go round!"*

~~Pastor Terrance Levise Turner, MBA

Gain 20/20 Vision For The New Decade!
2022 – 365 Day Journal
Document Your Journey!

Living Proverb #1670: *"If you set big goals, you'll accomplish big things. If you set small goals, you'll accomplish small things. If you set no goals, you'll accomplish nothing."*

~~**Pastor Terrance Levise Turner, MBA**

Gain 20/20 Vision For The New Decade!
2022 – 365 Day Journal
Document Your Journey!

Living Proverb #1671: *"People with purpose make the best students. You don't have to give them a reason to stay motivated, focused, and passionate."*

~~Pastor Terrance Levise Turner, MBA

Gain 20/20 Vision For The New Decade!
2022 – 365 Day Journal
Document Your Journey!

Living Proverb #1673: *"The sign of a true entrepreneur is the ability to create great things out of limited resources."*

~~**Pastor Terrance Levise Turner, MBA**

Gain 20/20 Vision For The New Decade!
2022 – 365 Day Journal
Document Your Journey!

Living Proverb #1674: *"The key to maintaining our peace is to learn to live an uncomplicated life in the midst of a very complicated world."*

~~**Pastor Terrance Levise Turner, MBA**

Gain 20/20 Vision For The New Decade!
2022 – 365 Day Journal
Document Your Journey!

Living Proverb #1675: *"You must win the inner battle before you can win the outer battle."*

~~**Pastor Terrance Levise Turner, MBA**

Gain 20/20 Vision For The New Decade!
2022 – 365 Day Journal
Document Your Journey!

Living Proverb #1676: *"If you would like a fresh start to your mental day, take time to read five or ten chapters of one of the four gospels, Matthew, Mark, Luke, or John."*

~~**Pastor Terrance Levise Turner, MBA**

Gain 20/20 Vision For The New Decade!
2022 – 365 Day Journal
Document Your Journey!

Living Proverb #1680: *"One word from God can open your eyes from being "future–blind" and almost hopeless, to being passionately focused and hopeful for your future."*

~~**Pastor Terrance Levise Turner, MBA**

Gain 20/20 Vision For The New Decade!
2022 – 365 Day Journal
Document Your Journey!

Living Proverb #1681: *"Faith is admirable."*

~~Pastor Terrance Levise Turner, MBA

Gain 20/20 Vision For The New Decade!
2022 – 365 Day Journal
Document Your Journey!

Living Proverb #1682: *"If your money doesn't have a specific place to go, it will go."*

~~**Pastor Terrance Levise Turner, MBA**

Gain 20/20 Vision For The New Decade!
2022 – 365 Day Journal
Document Your Journey!

Living Proverb #1684: *"Ask people nicely, and they will do more for you so much easier."*

~~Pastor Terrance Levise Turner, MBA

Gain 20/20 Vision For The New Decade!
2022 – 365 Day Journal
Document Your Journey!

Living Proverb #1685: *"Once you reach a certain level of maturity, God expects you to rule yourself. He expects you to rule your own time, eating habits, work habits, and all of your life."*

~~**Pastor Terrance Levise Turner, MBA**

Gain 20/20 Vision For The New Decade!
2022 – 365 Day Journal
Document Your Journey!

Living Proverb #1687: *"The greatest teachers are profitable practitioners of their lessons learned. They are proof positive of their wisdom gained."*

~~Pastor Terrance Levise Turner, MBA

Gain 20/20 Vision For The New Decade!
2022 – 365 Day Journal
Document Your Journey!

Living Proverb #1689: *"Opportunity is a walking Man. If you don't stop Him to sit down and have dinner, and to hear Him speak, He will keep walking on by."*

~~**Pastor Terrance Levise Turner, MBA**

Gain 20/20 Vision For The New Decade!
2022 – 365 Day Journal
Document Your Journey!

Living Proverb #1691: *"God prepares you for life. If you keep on walking by faith, you'll be prepared for the next leg of the race."*

~~Pastor Terrance Levise Turner, MBA

Gain 20/20 Vision For The New Decade!
2022 – 365 Day Journal
Document Your Journey!

Living Proverb #1692a: *"Go with the flow of favor in life, because you don't know what the future will hold. You will need it. Go with the flow of favor."*

~~**Pastor Terrance Levise Turner, MBA**

Gain 20/20 Vision For The New Decade!
2022 – 365 Day Journal
Document Your Journey!

Living Proverb #1692b: *"Do the right thing when it's the right time, and you will have the right harvest at the right time."*

~~Pastor Terrance Levise Turner, MBA

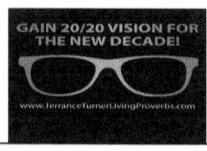

Gain 20/20 Vision For The New Decade!
2022 – 365 Day Journal
Document Your Journey!

Living Proverb #1694: *"The greatest thing that you can do for your family is to be successful. Abraham had to leave his family to go and succeed. Isaac succeeded. Jacob went and succeeded."*

~~**Pastor Terrance Levise Turner, MBA**

Gain 20/20 Vision For The New Decade!
2022 – 365 Day Journal
Document Your Journey!

Living Proverb #1699: *"We don't have to be threatened by artificial intelligence, which was programmed by human intelligence, which was imparted by Divine intelligence."*

~~**Pastor Terrance Levise Turner, MBA**

Gain 20/20 Vision For The New Decade!
2022 – 365 Day Journal
Document Your Journey!

Living Proverb #1700: *"Regarding doing the work of God, prepare like it all depended on you, but seek God like it all depended on Him."*

~~**Pastor Terrance Levise Turner, MBA**

Gain 20/20 Vision For The New Decade!
2022 – 365 Day Journal
Document Your Journey!

Living Proverb #1701: *"You may feel like you need to make more money, but if you focus on making more progress, you will make more money."*

~~**Pastor Terrance Levise Turner, MBA**

Gain 20/20 Vision For The New Decade!
2022 – 365 Day Journal
Document Your Journey!

Living Proverb #1705: *"You will always win a battle if you keep your peace."*

~~**Pastor Terrance Levise Turner, MBA**

Gain 20/20 Vision For The New Decade!
2022 – 365 Day Journal
Document Your Journey!

Living Proverb #1706: *"Keep your head up. Walk like a king. Stay up and never slide down. Be the victor and not the victim. And never let anybody put you on the back of the bus!"*

~~**Pastor Terrance Levise Turner, MBA**

Gain 20/20 Vision For The New Decade!
2022 – 365 Day Journal
Document Your Journey!

Living Proverb #1707: *"Respect for yourself and others will make for a respectable relationship."*

~~**Pastor Terrance Levise Turner, MBA**

Gain 20/20 Vision For The New Decade!
2022 – 365 Day Journal
Document Your Journey!

Living Proverb #1708: *"Here's a lesson: Never miss an opportunity to be a blessing to others, even when it takes courage to say something or do something. Always choose to be a blessing."*

~~Pastor Terrance Levise Turner, MBA

Gain 20/20 Vision For The New Decade!
2022 – 365 Day Journal
Document Your Journey!

Living Proverb #1709: *"Faith comes by hearing. Faith is the ability to take action. If you have not been taking enough action in life, you must take time to build up your faith."*

~~**Pastor Terrance Levise Turner, MBA**

Gain 20/20 Vision For The New Decade!
2022 – 365 Day Journal
Document Your Journey!

Living Proverb #1712: *"Creation is the first phase of profit. You can always sell something that you have. You can't sell something that you don't have. Creation is the first phase of profit."*
~~**Pastor Terrance Levise Turner, MBA**

Gain 20/20 Vision For The New Decade!
2022 – 365 Day Journal
Document Your Journey!

Living Proverb #1713: *"Nobody is concerned about doing what you need to do, but you. If you don't do it, it won't get done. If you don't run your race, it won't be run."*

~~**Pastor Terrance Levise Turner, MBA**

Gain 20/20 Vision For The New Decade!
2022 – 365 Day Journal
Document Your Journey!

Living Proverb #1714: *"Do big things and you will become larger. Do even more big things, and you will become larger even faster."*
~~Pastor Terrance Levise Turner, MBA

Gain 20/20 Vision For The New Decade!
2022 – 365 Day Journal
Document Your Journey!

Living Proverb #1715: *"Knowledge comes from learning and study. Growing comes from doing."*

~~Pastor Terrance Levise Turner, MBA

Gain 20/20 Vision For The New Decade!
2022 – 365 Day Journal
Document Your Journey!

Living Proverb #1716: *"When life becomes confusing, pray in the Holy Ghost. Pray out the answers to those mysteries."*
~~**Pastor Terrance Levise Turner, MBA**

Gain 20/20 Vision For The New Decade!
2022 – 365 Day Journal
Document Your Journey!

Living Proverb #1717: *"What would history be called if women ruled the world? It would be called her–story!"*

~~**Pastor Terrance Levise Turner, MBA**

Gain 20/20 Vision For The New Decade!
2022 – 365 Day Journal
Document Your Journey!

Living Proverb #1718: *"Don't listen to "loser talk", even if it's coming from a winner. Rather, pay attention to what the winner is doing and follow their example, and you'll become a winner too!"*

~~Pastor Terrance Levise Turner, MBA

Gain 20/20 Vision For The New Decade!
2022 – 365 Day Journal
Document Your Journey!

Living Proverb #1719a: *"Regarding sales, continue to create excellence, and be productive, rather than overly focusing on the sales process. You can always sell something that you have."*

~~**Pastor Terrance Levise Turner, MBA**

Gain 20/20 Vision For The New Decade!
2022 – 365 Day Journal
Document Your Journey!

Living Proverb #1719b: *"Focus on being productive and excellent, just like every successful innovator, and then the sales process will be able to be taken care of on its own."*

~~**Pastor Terrance Levise Turner, MBA**

Gain 20/20 Vision For The New Decade!
2022 – 365 Day Journal
Document Your Journey!

___

Living Proverb #1720: *"Close the circle of productivity with profit."*

~~**Pastor Terrance Levise Turner, MBA**

Gain 20/20 Vision For The New Decade!
2022 – 365 Day Journal
Document Your Journey!

Living Proverb #1721: *"Favor plus labor equals success."*
~~Pastor Terrance Levise Turner, MBA

Gain 20/20 Vision For The New Decade!
2022 – 365 Day Journal
Document Your Journey!

Living Proverb #1722: *"Success may be slow, but true success is sure, if you keep working on the right things in the right way overtime. Success may be slow, but true success is sure."*

~~**Pastor Terrance Levise Turner, MBA**

Gain 20/20 Vision For The New Decade!
2022 – 365 Day Journal
Document Your Journey!

Living Proverb #1723: *"Life takes faith and trust. It takes faith to go forward, and trust to be patient in the process."*
~~**Pastor Terrance Levise Turner, MBA**

Gain 20/20 Vision For The New Decade!
2022 – 365 Day Journal
Document Your Journey!

Living Proverb #1724: *"May you demonstrate the style of a victor, and not a victim: a winner and not a whiner. Greater is He who is in you, than he that is in the world."*

~~**Pastor Terrance Levise Turner, MBA**

Gain 20/20 Vision For The New Decade!
2022 – 365 Day Journal
Document Your Journey!

Living Proverb #1725: *"A life built upon truth appreciates in value over time. A life built upon falsehood declines and depreciates in value over time."*

~~**Pastor Terrance Levise Turner, MBA**

Gain 20/20 Vision For The New Decade!
2022 – 365 Day Journal
Document Your Journey!

Living Proverb #1726: *"Patience and planning are the keys to financial freedom. Impatience and impulsiveness are the keys to continued poverty."*

~~**Pastor Terrance Levise Turner, MBA**

Gain 20/20 Vision For The New Decade!
2022 – 365 Day Journal
Document Your Journey!

Living Proverb #1734: *"People who get it done like to work with people who get it done."*

~~Pastor Terrance Levise Turner, MBA

Gain 20/20 Vision For The New Decade!
2022 – 365 Day Journal
Document Your Journey!

Living Proverb #1737: *"Both fear and faith are alternate states of reality. Take time to dwell in the alternate state of faith, and you will change your reality."*

~~Pastor Terrance Levise Turner, MBA

Gain 20/20 Vision For The New Decade!
2022 – 365 Day Journal
Document Your Journey!

Living Proverb #1738: *"When it's time for your blessing, God can compress time to get it to you. Time is not a factor when it's time for your blessing."*

~~**Pastor Terrance Levise Turner, MBA**

Gain 20/20 Vision For The New Decade!
2022 – 365 Day Journal
Document Your Journey!

Living Proverb #1744: *"God has enabled you. God has made you able. God has provided you with the means, opportunity, power, and authority to be successful. He's made it possible."*

~~**Pastor Terrance Levise Turner, MBA**

Gain 20/20 Vision For The New Decade!
2022 – 365 Day Journal
Document Your Journey!

Living Proverb #1748: *"Exercise, healthy food, and rest help the body and mind deal with stress, so that you can do your best. It helps you recalibrate."*

~~**Pastor Terrance Levise Turner, MBA**

Gain 20/20 Vision For The New Decade!
2022 – 365 Day Journal
Document Your Journey!

Living Proverb #1753: *"You must do what's required to obtain what's desired. What's required usually is much more than what you at first anticipated."*

~~**Pastor Terrance Levise Turner, MBA**

Gain 20/20 Vision For The New Decade!
2022 – 365 Day Journal
Document Your Journey!

Living Proverb #1759: *"Life is like a close race. The person who leans in will win. Lean in! Put your heart into the race!"*
~~Pastor Terrance Levise Turner, MBA

Gain 20/20 Vision For The New Decade!
2022 – 365 Day Journal
Document Your Journey!

Living Proverb #1760: *"Some things are better unsaid."*

~~Pastor Terrance Levise Turner, MBA

Gain 20/20 Vision For The New Decade!
2022 – 365 Day Journal
Document Your Journey!

Living Proverb #1761: *"A good friend is not afraid to tell you the truth."*

~~**Pastor Terrance Levise Turner, MBA**

Gain 20/20 Vision For The New Decade!
2022 – 365 Day Journal
Document Your Journey!

Living Proverb #1764: *"Success is achievable. You can obtain it if you train for it. You must prepare for success. You must run the race to win."*

~~**Pastor Terrance Levise Turner, MBA**

Gain 20/20 Vision For The New Decade!
2022 – 365 Day Journal
Document Your Journey!

Living Proverb #1765: *"Sometimes it's more glory for people to see you struggle and overcome, than to be able to act like you have no problems and fake people out. There's glory in your struggles."*

~~**Pastor Terrance Levise Turner, MBA**

Gain 20/20 Vision For The New Decade!
2022 – 365 Day Journal
Document Your Journey!

Living Proverb #1766: *"The best meals have plenty of flavor without being overly filling. The best conversations have plenty of meaning without an overuse of words."*

~~**Pastor Terrance Levise Turner, MBA**

Gain 20/20 Vision For The New Decade!
2022 – 365 Day Journal
Document Your Journey!

Living Proverb #1767: *"As you take care of others, be sure to take care of you, because no one will take care of you, like you're supposed to take care of you."*

~~**Pastor Terrance Levise Turner, MBA**

Gain 20/20 Vision For The New Decade!
2022 – 365 Day Journal
Document Your Journey!

Living Proverb #1769: *"You are an optimum, excellent, superior, outstanding, godly, exceptional person. You fulfill God's highest ideals. You're pleasing to God. He loves you very much."*

~~**Pastor Terrance Levise Turner, MBA**

Gain 20/20 Vision For The New Decade!
2022 – 365 Day Journal
Document Your Journey!

Living Proverb #1770: *"Listen to the customers, rather than listening to the experts. The customers are the experts."*
~~**Pastor Terrance Levise Turner, MBA**

Gain 20/20 Vision For The New Decade!
2022 – 365 Day Journal
Document Your Journey!

Living Proverb #1771: *"When you know you are a person of ideas that have appreciating value, be sure to know and be careful of the people you hook up with when you are on the ground floor."*

~~Pastor Terrance Levise Turner, MBA

Gain 20/20 Vision For The New Decade!
2022 – 365 Day Journal
Document Your Journey!

Living Proverb #1773a: *"In some circles, a new idea will be celebrated and exalted as very valuable. It may be considered priceless or worth $1 million or more."*

~~**Pastor Terrance Levise Turner, MBA**

Gain 20/20 Vision For The New Decade!
2022 – 365 Day Journal
Document Your Journey!

Living Proverb #1773b: *"In other circles, that same new idea will be passed by and counted as almost worthless."*

~~**Pastor Terrance Levise Turner, MBA**

Gain 20/20 Vision For The New Decade!
2022 – 365 Day Journal
Document Your Journey!

Living Proverb #1773c: *"Determination of the value of a new idea is usually determined by the size of the minds of the circle of people that it's introduced to."*

~~**Pastor Terrance Levise Turner, MBA**

Gain 20/20 Vision For The New Decade!
2022 – 365 Day Journal
Document Your Journey!

Living Proverb #1773d: *"Therefore, it's critical to choose the right circles when introducing a new idea."*
~~**Pastor Terrance Levise Turner, MBA**

Gain 20/20 Vision For The New Decade!
2022 – 365 Day Journal
Document Your Journey!

Living Proverb #1774: *"Every good man needs a good woman with fire in her engine, softness on her face, love in her heart, and intelligence in her brain, and to make her his wife."*

~~**Pastor Terrance Levise Turner, MBA**

Gain 20/20 Vision For The New Decade!
2022 – 365 Day Journal
Document Your Journey!

_____
_____
_____
_____
_____
_____
_____
_____
_____
_____
_____
_____
_____
_____
_____
_____
_____
_____
_____
_____
_____
_____
_____
_____
_____
_____
_____
_____
_____
_____
_____

Living Proverb #1775: *"Take precautions, and thus, save repairs."*
~~**Pastor Terrance Levise Turner, MBA**

Gain 20/20 Vision For The New Decade!
2022 – 365 Day Journal
Document Your Journey!

Living Proverb #1776: *"The only way to heal the other person is to heal you. Never hate another. Rather, love yourself. Thus, freeing you from the hatred or manipulation of another person."*

~~**Pastor Terrance Levise Turner, MBA**

Gain 20/20 Vision For The New Decade!
2022 – 365 Day Journal
Document Your Journey!

Living Proverb #1779: *"God's grace can help you deal with the real, and cause your life to go from being less than ideal to becoming fulfilled."*

~~**Pastor Terrance Levise Turner, MBA**

Gain 20/20 Vision For The New Decade!
2022 – 365 Day Journal
Document Your Journey!

Living Proverb #1780: *"Love is unfeigned commitment for an indefinite period of time. The commitment involves kindness, care, and the intentional betterment of the other person."*

~~**Pastor Terrance Levise Turner, MBA**

Gain 20/20 Vision For The New Decade!
2022 – 365 Day Journal
Document Your Journey!

Living Proverb #1783: *"Regarding progress, you don't need the approval of people who are not doing anything in life to help you go forward. Go forward!"*

~~**Pastor Terrance Levise Turner, MBA**

Gain 20/20 Vision For The New Decade!
2022 – 365 Day Journal
Document Your Journey!

Living Proverb #1784: *"Hold your peace, and don't let anyone steal it. Overcome evil with good. Overcome disorder with order. Overcome intimidation with calm confidence."*

~~**Pastor Terrance Levise Turner, MBA**

Gain 20/20 Vision For The New Decade!
2022 – 365 Day Journal
Document Your Journey!

Living Proverb #1785: *"If you ask anybody that is somebody how they became somebody, they will tell you that it took a lot of hard, smart work."*

~~**Pastor Terrance Levise Turner, MBA**

Gain 20/20 Vision For The New Decade!
2022 – 365 Day Journal
Document Your Journey!

Living Proverb #1787: *"Once you make up your mind to actually blast off in life, life itself will begin to throw gas on you to escalate your acceleration. Blast off! There is nothing hindering you!"*
~~**Pastor Terrance Levise Turner, MBA**

Gain 20/20 Vision For The New Decade!
2022 – 365 Day Journal
Document Your Journey!

Living Proverb #1788: *"What gets measured can be managed. Whether it's time, money, calories, steps, etc. What gets measured can be managed."*

~~**Pastor Terrance Levise Turner, MBA**

Gain 20/20 Vision For The New Decade!
2022 – 365 Day Journal
Document Your Journey!

Living Proverb #1789: *"Life can be eventful. Handle it with prayer."*

~~Pastor Terrance Levise Turner, MBA

Gain 20/20 Vision For The New Decade!
2022 – 365 Day Journal
Document Your Journey!

Living Proverb #1790: *"God always responds to faith. Prosperity always responds to order. You need faith and order to create and maintain prosperity."*

~~**Pastor Terrance Levise Turner, MBA**

Gain 20/20 Vision For The New Decade!
2022 – 365 Day Journal
Document Your Journey!

Living Proverb #1791: *"Whatever you're facing in this moment, God has grace for you. Grace is God's ability to do for you, in you, or through you what you can't do in your own natural strength."*

~~**Pastor Terrance Levise Turner, MBA**

Gain 20/20 Vision For The New Decade!
2022 – 365 Day Journal
Document Your Journey!

Living Proverb #1792: *"The first stage of profit is learning."*

~~Pastor Terrance Levise Turner, MBA

Gain 20/20 Vision For The New Decade!
2022 – 365 Day Journal
Document Your Journey!

Living Proverb #1793: *"The longer you wait the less gets accomplished. You've got to stay on the run, to get the job done."*
~~**Pastor Terrance Levise Turner, MBA**

Gain 20/20 Vision For The New Decade!
2022 – 365 Day Journal
Document Your Journey!

Living Proverb #1794: *"Singing praise and worship music releases endorphins and angels on your behalf. Take time to sing praise and worship. You will be blessed and protected."*

~~**Pastor Terrance Levise Turner, MBA**

Gain 20/20 Vision For The New Decade!
2022 – 365 Day Journal
Document Your Journey!

Living Proverb #1796: *"A lot of times you can get more answers by being quiet than you can by talking."*

~~Pastor Terrance Levise Turner, MBA

Gain 20/20 Vision For The New Decade!
2022 – 365 Day Journal
Document Your Journey!

Living Proverb #1795: *"There's rarely any drawback to keeping your mouth shut."*

~~Pastor Terrance Levise Turner, MBA

Gain 20/20 Vision For The New Decade!
2022 – 365 Day Journal
Document Your Journey!

Living Proverb #1797: *"Life is short. You've got to be patient."*
~~Pastor Terrance Levise Turner, MBA

Gain 20/20 Vision For The New Decade!
2022 – 365 Day Journal
Document Your Journey!

Living Proverb #1799: *"Never get so sophisticated that you can't say, 'Thank You Jesus!'"*

~~**Pastor Terrance Levise Turner, MBA**

Gain 20/20 Vision For The New Decade!
2022 – 365 Day Journal
Document Your Journey!

Living Proverb #1800: *"Life happens. You must be able to pivot."*
~~Pastor Terrance Levise Turner, MBA

Gain 20/20 Vision For The New Decade!
2022 – 365 Day Journal
Document Your Journey!

Living Proverb #1801: *"Prior to every meeting, always remember that every conversation was proceeded by a conversation. Therefore, never be careless in your conversations."*

~~**Pastor Terrance Levise Turner, MBA**

Gain 20/20 Vision For The New Decade!
2022 – 365 Day Journal
Document Your Journey!

Living Proverb #1802: *"When you have a destiny to accomplish, God is working harder than you are to make sure it comes to pass."*
~~**Pastor Terrance Levise Turner, MBA**

Gain 20/20 Vision For The New Decade!
2022 – 365 Day Journal
Document Your Journey!

Living Proverb #1804: *"There's more than one way of teaching. If you're a good student, then you are able to adjust your learning capacity to the specific lessons of life."*

~~**Pastor Terrance Levise Turner, MBA**

Gain 20/20 Vision For The New Decade!
2022 – 365 Day Journal
Document Your Journey!

Living Proverb #1805: *"Have a plan, yet, be open to the possibilities of God."*

~~**Pastor Terrance Levise Turner, MBA**

Gain 20/20 Vision For The New Decade!
2022 – 365 Day Journal
Document Your Journey!

Living Proverb #1806: *"Keep on producing with excellence. Make your own name. You won't need anyone else's name."*

~~**Pastor Terrance Levise Turner, MBA**

Gain 20/20 Vision For The New Decade!
2022 – 365 Day Journal
Document Your Journey!

Living Proverb #1807: *"When people can make you, then, people can break you. Do what God has called you to do. Pay the price to become qualified. Then, make your own luck."*

~~**Pastor Terrance Levise Turner, MBA**

Gain 20/20 Vision For The New Decade!
2022 – 365 Day Journal
Document Your Journey!

Living Proverb #1808: *"When you know your own value, you won't cheapen your asking price."*

~~**Pastor Terrance Levise Turner, MBA**

Gain 20/20 Vision For The New Decade!
2022 – 365 Day Journal
Document Your Journey!

Living Proverb #1809: *"Don't spend your time tending to someone else's business. Rather, spend your time tending to your own business, because, that's what's going to pay you."*

~~**Pastor Terrance Levise Turner, MBA**

Gain 20/20 Vision For The New Decade!
2022 – 365 Day Journal
Document Your Journey!

Living Proverb #1810: *"Regarding creating a future for your family, Go ahead! Somebody has to go ahead in order to create a prosperous posterity for your family. Don't be afraid to be the first."*

~~**Pastor Terrance Levise Turner, MBA**

Gain 20/20 Vision For The New Decade!
2022 – 365 Day Journal
Document Your Journey!

Living Proverb #1811b: *"Satisfaction comes from accomplishing great deeds, whether large or small. Salvation is by grace, through faith. Satisfaction is by accomplishing what God created you to do."*
~~Pastor Terrance Levise Turner, MBA

Gain 20/20 Vision For The New Decade!
2022 – 365 Day Journal
Document Your Journey!

Living Proverb #1814: *"You can't hide quality, and you can't really fake it. You must develop it. Be the best at what God made you to do and be by continual self–development."*

~~**Pastor Terrance Levise Turner, MBA**

Gain 20/20 Vision For The New Decade!
2022 – 365 Day Journal
Document Your Journey!

Living Proverb #1819: *"If we will restrict our diets while we are free to choose, we won't be forced to restrict our diets."*
~~Pastor Terrance Levise Turner, MBA

Gain 20/20 Vision For The New Decade!
2022 – 365 Day Journal
Document Your Journey!

Living Proverb #1820: *"We often miss potential miracles, because we fail to notice and value the flowers that grow in between the cracks of time. Every miracle may not happen on your schedule."*

~~**Pastor Terrance Levise Turner, MBA**

Gain 20/20 Vision For The New Decade!
2022 – 365 Day Journal
Document Your Journey!

Living Proverb #1821: *"In life, you have to take opportunities! They're not just handed to you. You must take opportunities for rest, recreation, idea creation, advancement, etc."*

*~~***Pastor Terrance Levise Turner, MBA***

Gain 20/20 Vision For The New Decade!
2022 – 365 Day Journal
Document Your Journey!

Living Proverb #1822: *"Regarding success, if you haven't succeeded, it's because you haven't done your best. Either, there's a lack of knowledge or a lack of action on the knowledge you have."*
~~**Pastor Terrance Levise Turner, MBA**

Gain 20/20 Vision For The New Decade!
2022 – 365 Day Journal
Document Your Journey!

Living Proverb #1823: *"Don't settle for defeat! Keep striving to do your best, in spite of setbacks or opposition! There's more in you than you know! Don't settle for defeat! Keep striving for the best!"*
~~**Pastor Terrance Levise Turner, MBA**

Gain 20/20 Vision For The New Decade!
2022 – 365 Day Journal
Document Your Journey!

Living Proverb #1824: *"Challenges make champions better!"*

~~**Pastor Terrance Levise Turner, MBA**

Gain 20/20 Vision For The New Decade!
2022 – 365 Day Journal
Document Your Journey!

Living Proverb #1825: *"God doesn't bring His Word down to our performance. He brings His grace down to our performance, in order to help us come up to the standards of His Word."*
~~**Pastor Terrance Levise Turner, MBA**

Gain 20/20 Vision For The New Decade!
2022 – 365 Day Journal
Document Your Journey!

Living Proverb #1826: *"Regarding success, it's about execution. And, it's not over until the cash register sings!"*
~~**Pastor Terrance Levise Turner, MBA**

Gain 20/20 Vision For The New Decade!
2022 – 365 Day Journal
Document Your Journey!

Living Proverb #1827: *"Be the CEO of your own life. Set your own goals. Set your own deadlines. Then, do what's necessary to accomplish them. Be accountable to yourself. Be your own boss!"*

*~~***Pastor Terrance Levise Turner, MBA***

Gain 20/20 Vision For The New Decade!
2022 – 365 Day Journal
Document Your Journey!

Living Proverb #1828: *"Jump–start your day with a song of praise! Recognize God as the "Author" of your new day! Give Him thanksgiving for blessing you in all your ways."*

~~**Pastor Terrance Levise Turner, MBA**

Gain 20/20 Vision For The New Decade!
2022 – 365 Day Journal
Document Your Journey!

Living Proverb #1832: *"Learn a lesson from the birds: talk to and praise God early in the morning."*
~~Pastor Terrance Levise Turner, MBA

Gain 20/20 Vision For The New Decade!
2022 – 365 Day Journal
Document Your Journey!

Living Proverb #1834: *"Most people are full of excuses today, and full of regrets tomorrow. Take action today, and you'll be happier tomorrow."*

~~**Pastor Terrance Levise Turner, MBA**

Gain 20/20 Vision For The New Decade!
2022 – 365 Day Journal
Document Your Journey!

Living Proverb #1835: *"You're smart! Don't be afraid to keep your own counsel, because nothing was ever the right way of doing something, until someone successfully did it"*

~~**Pastor Terrance Levise Turner, MBA**

Gain 20/20 Vision For The New Decade!
2022 – 365 Day Journal
Document Your Journey!

Living Proverb #1836: *"Don't be afraid to be uncommon. Only through your acknowledgement of the fact that you are uncommon, will you be able to properly give your uncommon gift to the world"*
~~**Pastor Terrance Levise Turner, MBA**

Gain 20/20 Vision For The New Decade!
2022 – 365 Day Journal
Document Your Journey!

Living Proverb #1837: *"When you submit your will to God's will, there's nothing in Earth, Heaven, or in Hell that can withstand the force of that will. It shall come to pass."*

~~**Pastor Terrance Levise Turner, MBA**

Gain 20/20 Vision For The New Decade!
2022 – 365 Day Journal
Document Your Journey!

Living Proverb #1838: *"Never replace the brand of God for the brand of man. God brands your heart. Man attempts to brand your mind. Take time to renew your mind with the Word of God."*

~~**Pastor Terrance Levise Turner, MBA**

Gain 20/20 Vision For The New Decade!
2022 – 365 Day Journal
Document Your Journey!

Living Proverb #1842: *"True love doesn't require you to let yourself be abused. That would not be true love. True love begins with you loving you."*

~~**Pastor Terrance Levise Turner, MBA**

Gain 20/20 Vision For The New Decade!
2022 – 365 Day Journal
Document Your Journey!

Living Proverb #1848: *"Without action there's no satisfaction. Without action there are no results. Without action there's no fulfillment of the promise!"*

~~Pastor Terrance Levise Turner, MBA

Gain 20/20 Vision For The New Decade!
2022 – 365 Day Journal
Document Your Journey!

Living Proverb #1850: *"Be your own cheerleader! Only you are responsible to know exactly what it takes to motivate you. Don't put that responsibility on anyone else."*

~~**Pastor Terrance Levise Turner, MBA**

Gain 20/20 Vision For The New Decade!
2022 – 365 Day Journal
Document Your Journey!

Living Proverb #1851: *"Success takes what it takes. Don't be afraid or discouraged by the time that it takes to succeed. You don't have anything else to do, but fail, if you don't go for it! So, go for it!"*

*~~***Pastor Terrance Levise Turner, MBA***

Gain 20/20 Vision For The New Decade!
2022 – 365 Day Journal
Document Your Journey!

Living Proverb #1854: *"Success is not overnight. However, success is every night. To achieve and maintain success takes every day and every night."*

~~**Pastor Terrance Levise Turner, MBA**

Gain 20/20 Vision For The New Decade!
2022 – 365 Day Journal
Document Your Journey!

Living Proverb #1855: *"Pay off your small credit cards as soon as possible, because the "small foxes" spoil the credit!"*

~~**Pastor Terrance Levise Turner, MBA**

Gain 20/20 Vision For The New Decade!
2022 – 365 Day Journal
Document Your Journey!

Living Proverb #1863: *"People who have extra did extra."*
~~Pastor Terrance Levise Turner, MBA

Gain 20/20 Vision For The New Decade!
2022 – 365 Day Journal
Document Your Journey!

Living Proverb #1864: *"No one person or group of people has the monopoly on good ideas. The only person who has a monopoly on good ideas is the one who takes action on those ideas."*

~~**Pastor Terrance Levise Turner, MBA**

Gain 20/20 Vision For The New Decade!
2022 – 365 Day Journal
Document Your Journey!

Living Proverb #1867: *"Some people love you just because. Some people love you because. Always know the difference, and know that true love is a free gift."*

~~**Pastor Terrance Levise Turner, MBA**

Gain 20/20 Vision For The New Decade!
2022 – 365 Day Journal
Document Your Journey!

Living Proverb #1869: *"After you've had a long day, the habit of meditating the Word of God will reconstitute you into a full, whole, strong man or woman."*

~~Pastor Terrance Levise Turner, MBA

Gain 20/20 Vision For The New Decade!
2022 – 365 Day Journal
Document Your Journey!

Living Proverb #1870: *"The Word of God will transform you."*
~~Pastor Terrance Levise Turner, MBA

Gain 20/20 Vision For The New Decade!
2022 – 365 Day Journal
Document Your Journey!

Living Proverb #1871: *"Do not be conformed to this world and its way of thinking. Rather, be a transformer! Transform your mind by the Word of God! Meditate God's Word daily."*

~~Pastor Terrance Levise Turner, MBA

Gain 20/20 Vision For The New Decade!
2022 – 365 Day Journal
Document Your Journey!

Living Proverb #1875: *"As you feed upon God's Word, by actively, intentionally using it as a tool to advance in life, you will discover new levels of productivity."*

~~Pastor Terrance Levise Turner, MBA

Gain 20/20 Vision For The New Decade!
2022 – 365 Day Journal
Document Your Journey!

Living Proverb #1878: *"Read the Bible everyday. Pray everyday. Sing songs of worship to God everyday."*

~~**Pastor Terrance Levise Turner, MBA**

Gain 20/20 Vision For The New Decade!
2022 – 365 Day Journal
Document Your Journey!

Living Proverb #1879: *"Unreleased potential fails to benefit you."*
~~Pastor Terrance Levise Turner, MBA

Gain 20/20 Vision For The New Decade!
2022 – 365 Day Journal
Document Your Journey!

Living Proverb #1880: *"Life is a collection of moments. Whether in marriage, conversations, sports, enjoying meals, coffee, tea, etc. Savor the moments, and make the most of your life!"*

~~**Pastor Terrance Levise Turner, MBA**

Gain 20/20 Vision For The New Decade!
2022 – 365 Day Journal
Document Your Journey!

Living Proverb #1881: *"If you're patient enough, and you give yourself enough learning time, you can eliminate begging. Begging is a result of lack. It's a result of lack of knowledge."*

~~**Pastor Terrance Levise Turner, MBA**

Gain 20/20 Vision For The New Decade!
2022 – 365 Day Journal
Document Your Journey!

Living Proverb #1883: *"Keep on praying, because, everyday anything is possible through the grace of God."*
~~**Pastor Terrance Levise Turner, MBA**

Gain 20/20 Vision For The New Decade!
2022 – 365 Day Journal
Document Your Journey!

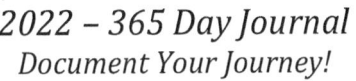

Living Proverb #1884: *"To go through a day "prayer–less" is perilous!"*

~~Pastor Terrance Levise Turner, MBA

Gain 20/20 Vision For The New Decade!
2022 – 365 Day Journal
Document Your Journey!

Living Proverb #1885: *"Marriage is honorable, and the bed is undefiled; but whoremongers and adulterers God will judge. We should honor the marriage covenant between a man and a woman."*

~~**Pastor Terrance Levise Turner, MBA**

Gain 20/20 Vision For The New Decade!
2022 – 365 Day Journal
Document Your Journey!

Living Proverb #1886: *"When God tells you to do something, just obey. It doesn't have to be pretty for it to be effective. If He tells you to do it, just quickly obey."*

~~Pastor Terrance Levise Turner, MBA

Gain 20/20 Vision For The New Decade!
2022 – 365 Day Journal
Document Your Journey!

Living Proverb #1887: *"A person that can control his or her own-self can control the world, and that scares some people."*

~~**Pastor Terrance Levise Turner, MBA**

Gain 20/20 Vision For The New Decade!
2022 – 365 Day Journal
Document Your Journey!

Living Proverb #1889: *"Make productivity a priority above publicity. Productivity is the key, because if you don't have anything to sell, then you don't have anything to promote."*

~~Pastor Terrance Levise Turner, MBA

Gain 20/20 Vision For The New Decade!
2022 – 365 Day Journal
Document Your Journey!

Living Proverb #1890: *"Do a great job! And, congratulate yourself often. Because, often you may be your only cheerleader in the whole universe!"*

~~**Pastor Terrance Levise Turner, MBA**

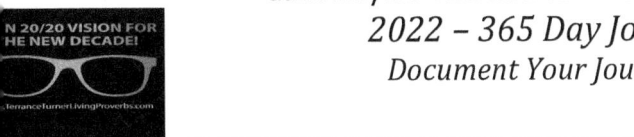

Gain 20/20 Vision For The New Decade!
2022 – 365 Day Journal
Document Your Journey!

Living Proverb #1891: *"The key to maintaining joy is to focus on the good, and to be thankful!"*
~~Pastor Terrance Levise Turner, MBA

Gain 20/20 Vision For The New Decade!
2022 – 365 Day Journal
Document Your Journey!

Living Proverb #1892: *"There's safety in following in someone else's footsteps. However, it's better to have your own boots! Be wise enough to strike out on your own path! Make your own footsteps!"*

~~Pastor Terrance Levise Turner, MBA

Gain 20/20 Vision For The New Decade!
2022 – 365 Day Journal
Document Your Journey!

Living Proverb #1893: *"Be sober. Be vigilant. Don't let your emotions get the best of your head."*

~~Pastor Terrance Levise Turner, MBA

Gain 20/20 Vision For The New Decade!
2022 – 365 Day Journal
Document Your Journey!

Living Proverb #1894: *"Without discipline, there is no release. Without the release of the anointing, there is no wealth."*
~~Pastor Terrance Levise Turner, MBA

Gain 20/20 Vision For The New Decade!
2022 – 365 Day Journal
Document Your Journey!

Living Proverb #1895: *"Vision provokes passion! Through passion purpose is obtained. Passion is the ignition for movement. Without movement nothing is accomplished."*

*~~***Pastor Terrance Levise Turner, MBA***

Gain 20/20 Vision For The New Decade!
2022 – 365 Day Journal
Document Your Journey!

Living Proverb #1897: *"Some of the greatest blessings come out of service."*

~~Pastor Terrance Levise Turner, MBA

Gain 20/20 Vision For The New Decade!
2022 – 365 Day Journal
Document Your Journey!

Living Proverb #1898: *"Neither give place to the devil. Don't give him any room when you see a storm rising. Whether the storm is in the natural weather or in the spiritual, resist the devil."*

~~**Pastor Terrance Levise Turner, MBA**

Gain 20/20 Vision For The New Decade!
2022 – 365 Day Journal
Document Your Journey!

Living Proverb #1899: *"The best way to mark your calendar is through achieved goals. Keep your calendar full, by setting high, achievable goals, and keeping on achieving them."*

~~**Pastor Terrance Levise Turner, MBA**

Gain 20/20 Vision For The New Decade!
2022 – 365 Day Journal
Document Your Journey!

Living Proverb #1901: *"God wants to bless you, so that you'll help Him accomplish His purpose in the earth. We deprive Him of pleasure, and hinder His plan, when we fail to achieve."*

~~**Pastor Terrance Levise Turner, MBA**

Gain 20/20 Vision For The New Decade!
2022 – 365 Day Journal
Document Your Journey!

Living Proverb #1902: *"The only thing that stands between you and your greatest dreams coming true is work. The only thing that stands between you doing the work is your willingness."*

*~~***Pastor Terrance Levise Turner, MBA***

Gain 20/20 Vision For The New Decade!
2022 – 365 Day Journal
Document Your Journey!

Living Proverb #1903: *"Unbroken focus is the key to your ultimate financial success. Unending distractions are the keys to your eventual financial destruction."*

~~**Pastor Terrance Levise Turner, MBA**

Gain 20/20 Vision For The New Decade!
2022 – 365 Day Journal
Document Your Journey!

Living Proverb #1913: *"Everyone is a "star" in someone else's sky. So, shine while you can. Shine as bright as the Sun in the day. Give direction and guidance as the North Star in someone's night."*

~~**Pastor Terrance Levise Turner, MBA**

Gain 20/20 Vision For The New Decade!
2022 - 365 Day Journal
Document Your Journey!

Living Proverb #1914: *"Have a "spiritual sandwich" everyday. Have a morning devotion and an evening devotion. Talk to the Lord and praise Him in the middle of the day. You will never go hungry."*
~~Pastor Terrance Levise Turner, MBA

Gain 20/20 Vision For The New Decade!
2022 – 365 Day Journal
Document Your Journey!

Living Proverb #1915: *"God is pleased with you today! You are the highlight of Heaven. Every morning you wake up He delights in you. He takes pleasure in your progress, and in prospering you."*

~~**Pastor Terrance Levise Turner, MBA**

Gain 20/20 Vision For The New Decade!
2022 – 365 Day Journal
Document Your Journey!

Living Proverb #1916: *"Singing praise and worship to God clears out all of the cobwebs out of your mind and heart. Make room for the Holy Ghost. Sing praise and worship onto God."*

~~**Pastor Terrance Levise Turner, MBA**

Gain 20/20 Vision For The New Decade!
2022 – 365 Day Journal
Document Your Journey!

Living Proverb #1917: *"Singing daily is an attitude lifter!"*
~~**Pastor Terrance Levise Turner, MBA**

Gain 20/20 Vision For The New Decade!
2022 – 365 Day Journal
Document Your Journey!

Living Proverb #1918: *"Death is downward. Life is upward! Choose life! Choose to have a positive attitude. Think up! Speak up! Get up! And be up! Choose life. Choose a positive attitude."*
~~**Pastor Terrance Levise Turner, MBA**

Gain 20/20 Vision For The New Decade!
2022 – 365 Day Journal
Document Your Journey!

Living Proverb #1920: *"Regarding your field of dreams, you can't guarantee that if you build it, they will come, but you can guarantee that if you don't build it they won't come. Pursue your dreams."*

~~**Pastor Terrance Levise Turner, MBA**

Gain 20/20 Vision For The New Decade!
2022 – 365 Day Journal
Document Your Journey!

Living Proverb #1923: *"Some characteristics are a matter of personality. Some characteristics are a matter of refinement. Success requires refinement of our personalities."*

*~~***Pastor Terrance Levise Turner, MBA***

Gain 20/20 Vision For The New Decade!
2022 – 365 Day Journal
Document Your Journey!

Living Proverb #1926: *"Determination, patience, and persistence are the keys to success. Determine your desired destination. Be patient. Persist to the end, and you will obtain success."*

*~~***Pastor Terrance Levise Turner, MBA***

Gain 20/20 Vision For The New Decade!
2022 – 365 Day Journal
Document Your Journey!

Living Proverb #1927: *"Workers get paid by the hour. Producers get paid by the product. Workers earn a wage. Producers earn wealth."*

~~**Pastor Terrance Levise Turner, MBA**

Gain 20/20 Vision For The New Decade!
2022 – 365 Day Journal
Document Your Journey!

Living Proverb #1929: *"No matter how your critics try to fight you, always know that no one can fight what God has ordained. If God said, "Yes", who else matters?"*

*~~***Pastor Terrance Levise Turner, MBA**

Gain 20/20 Vision For The New Decade!
2022 – 365 Day Journal
Document Your Journey!

Living Proverb #1930: *"Take all opportunities that advance you in the right direction."*

~~Pastor Terrance Levise Turner, MBA

Gain 20/20 Vision For The New Decade!
2022 – 365 Day Journal
Document Your Journey!

Living Proverb #1933: *"Life takes courage."*

~~Pastor Terrance Levise Turner, MBA

Gain 20/20 Vision For The New Decade!
2022 – 365 Day Journal
Document Your Journey!

Living Proverb #1934: *"Regarding money, excitement leads to spending. Patience leads to planning. Be strategic in your use of money. It will lead to an exciting result!"*

~~**Pastor Terrance Levise Turner, MBA**

Gain 20/20 Vision For The New Decade!
2022 – 365 Day Journal
Document Your Journey!

Living Proverb #1935: *"Pay for advisement, but keep your own counsel!"*

*~~***Pastor Terrance Levise Turner, MBA***

Gain 20/20 Vision For The New Decade!
2022 – 365 Day Journal
Document Your Journey!

Living Proverb #1936: *"Always remember that you are the CEO of your own life. Pay for advice, but don't lose your status."*
~~Pastor Terrance Levise Turner, MBA

Gain 20/20 Vision For The New Decade!
2022 – 365 Day Journal
Document Your Journey!

Living Proverb #1937: *"Even a rattlesnake will slow down long enough for you to pet and comfort it when it's sick. But, don't fail to listen for the moving of its rattle again!"*

~~**Pastor Terrance Levise Turner, MBA**

Gain 20/20 Vision For The New Decade!
2022 – 365 Day Journal
Document Your Journey!

Living Proverb #1938a: *"Ideas and concepts are how the "West was won" and how business is run. Take time to appraise the tremendous monetary value of your own ideas and concepts!"*

*~~***Pastor Terrance Levise Turner, MBA***

Gain 20/20 Vision For The New Decade!
2022 – 365 Day Journal
Document Your Journey!

Living Proverb #1938b: *"Don't allow yourself to be swindled, hornswoggled, or bamboozled by others who will readily relieve you of the value you have produced if you fail to protect it!"*

~~**Pastor Terrance Levise Turner, MBA**

Gain 20/20 Vision For The New Decade!
2022 – 365 Day Journal
Document Your Journey!

Living Proverb #1939: *"Excitement begets spending. Patience begets planning."*

~~Pastor Terrance Levise Turner, MBA

Gain 20/20 Vision For The New Decade!
2022 – 365 Day Journal
Document Your Journey!

Living Proverb #1940: *"The way to succeed is to start with a burning, grand vision. Then, keep taking steps towards its fulfillment. It becomes clearer as you take actions towards it."*

~~**Pastor Terrance Levise Turner, MBA**

Gain 20/20 Vision For The New Decade!
2022 – 365 Day Journal
Document Your Journey!

Living Proverb #1941: *"When the saints prevail in prayer, the saints will prevail."*
~~Pastor Terrance Levise Turner, MBA

Gain 20/20 Vision For The New Decade!
2022 – 365 Day Journal
Document Your Journey!

Living Proverb #1942a: *"The best way to make money is to not spend money. There's a difference between an expense and an investment. Expenses are spent. Investments increase your future."*

*~~***Pastor Terrance Levise Turner, MBA**

Gain 20/20 Vision For The New Decade!
2022 – 365 Day Journal
Document Your Journey!

Living Proverb #1942b: *"Invest money and reduce the instances of spending money, and thus, you will make money."*

~~Pastor Terrance Levise Turner, MBA

Gain 20/20 Vision For The New Decade!
2022 – 365 Day Journal
Document Your Journey!

Living Proverb #1943: *"Invest your money to make more money. Don't just spend money randomly."*

~~**Pastor Terrance Levise Turner, MBA**

Gain 20/20 Vision For The New Decade!
2022 – 365 Day Journal
Document Your Journey!

Living Proverb #1944: *"Don't start spending before you start counting!"*

~~Pastor Terrance Levise Turner, MBA

Gain 20/20 Vision For The New Decade!
2022 – 365 Day Journal
Document Your Journey!

Living Proverb #1945: *"Don't worry about the time that it takes to do what's required to obtain what's desired. Progress is progressive."*

~~**Pastor Terrance Levise Turner, MBA**

Gain 20/20 Vision For The New Decade!
2022 – 365 Day Journal
Document Your Journey!

Living Proverb #1946: *"Life is full of reality. It's good to have a dream. The just shall live by his or her faith!"*

~~**Pastor Terrance Levise Turner, MBA**

Gain 20/20 Vision For The New Decade!
2022 – 365 Day Journal
Document Your Journey!

Living Proverb #1949: *"Life is a trip! Your attitude will determine how you take it!"*

~~Pastor Terrance Levise Turner, MBA

Gain 20/20 Vision For The New Decade!
2022 – 365 Day Journal
Document Your Journey!

Living Proverb #1950: *"Happiness and joy are a matter of choice. It's a matter of attitude. It's a matter of the heart. It's not a matter of the circumstances. Don't let anything or anyone take your joy."*
~~**Pastor Terrance Levise Turner, MBA**

Gain 20/20 Vision For The New Decade!
2022 – 365 Day Journal
Document Your Journey!

Living Proverb #1952: *"You're paid to solve problems. So, if you run away from problems, you're run away from your paycheck."*
~~**Pastor Terrance Levise Turner, MBA**

Gain 20/20 Vision For The New Decade!
2022 – 365 Day Journal
Document Your Journey!

Living Proverb #1953: *"The willingness to go to any lawful extreme is the price of extreme success."*

~~Pastor Terrance Levise Turner, MBA

Gain 20/20 Vision For The New Decade!
2022 – 365 Day Journal
Document Your Journey!

Living Proverb #1954: *"Drown out the voices of adversaries, opposition, and criticism by the force of your productivity."*

~~Pastor Terrance Levise Turner, MBA

Gain 20/20 Vision For The New Decade!
2022 – 365 Day Journal
Document Your Journey!

Living Proverb #1955: *"Keep sowing seed toward the future, and you will have both a future and a harvest."*

~~Pastor Terrance Levise Turner, MBA

Gain 20/20 Vision For The New Decade!
2022 – 365 Day Journal
Document Your Journey!

Living Proverb #1956: *"Regarding business, no single company or organization fully owns the entire market. Otherwise, they wouldn't continue marketing."*

*~~***Pastor Terrance Levise Turner, MBA***

Gain 20/20 Vision For The New Decade!
2022 – 365 Day Journal
Document Your Journey!

Living Proverb #1957: *"Don't fight getting older. Rather, focus on getting better every day of every year. Live with intentionality, so that you are daily fulfilling your God-given purpose."*

~~Pastor Terrance Levise Turner, MBA

Gain 20/20 Vision For The New Decade!
2022 – 365 Day Journal
Document Your Journey!

Living Proverb #1958: *"Insist on being the best, and make no allowances for mediocrity."*

~~**Pastor Terrance Levise Turner, MBA**

Gain 20/20 Vision For The New Decade!
2022 – 365 Day Journal
Document Your Journey!

Living Proverb #1959: *"Everybody needs to stand on their own two feet if they can, because the resistance of standing builds strength."*

~~Pastor Terrance Levise Turner, MBA

Gain 20/20 Vision For The New Decade!
2022 – 365 Day Journal
Document Your Journey!

Living Proverb #1960: *"Regarding business, business is not black-and-white. Business is green."*

~~**Pastor Terrance Levise Turner, MBA**

Gain 20/20 Vision For The New Decade!
2022 – 365 Day Journal
Document Your Journey!

Living Proverb #1962: *"The Lord is working on your behalf. The future is brighter than you may now perceive. Keep looking up. The Sun is shining in your direction!"*

~~**Pastor Terrance Levise Turner, MBA**

Gain 20/20 Vision For The New Decade!
2022 – 365 Day Journal
Document Your Journey!

Living Proverb #1963: *"The truth is never intimidated by a lie. The truth is the truth. It cannot lie. The truth is the truth. It can't be denied. The truth is never intimidated by a lie."*

~~**Pastor Terrance Levise Turner, MBA**

Gain 20/20 Vision For The New Decade!
2022 – 365 Day Journal
Document Your Journey!

Living Proverb #1964: *"Don't stress-out. Rather, press into prayer."*

~~Pastor Terrance Levise Turner, MBA

Gain 20/20 Vision For The New Decade!
2022 – 365 Day Journal
Document Your Journey!

Living Proverb #1965: *"Sincere appreciation is always appreciated."*

*~~***Pastor Terrance Levise Turner, MBA**

Gain 20/20 Vision For The New Decade!
2022 – 365 Day Journal
Document Your Journey!

Living Proverb #1966: *"If it can be done, it should be done. You don't know what can be done, until you try. Don't say what can't be done, until you try. If it's possible, it should be done. You can do it!"*
~~**Pastor Terrance Levise Turner, MBA**

Gain 20/20 Vision For The New Decade!
2022 – 365 Day Journal
Document Your Journey!

Living Proverb #1967: *"Wherever you are you should learn something."*

~~**Pastor Terrance Levise Turner, MBA**

Gain 20/20 Vision For The New Decade!
2022 – 365 Day Journal
Document Your Journey!

Living Proverb #1968: *"It pays to be prepared and prompt. It costs to be lax and late."*

~~Pastor Terrance Levise Turner, MBA

Gain 20/20 Vision For The New Decade!
2022 – 365 Day Journal
Document Your Journey!

Living Proverb #1969: *"Regarding rest, even the Sun goes down at the end of the day. Take time to get your rest."*

~~**Pastor Terrance Levise Turner, MBA**

Gain 20/20 Vision For The New Decade!
2022 – 365 Day Journal
Document Your Journey!

Living Proverb #1970a: *"Once you make the decision to solve a problem, it's no longer a problem. It becomes a challenge. Go forward courageously with the commitment to take the challenge."*

*~~***Pastor Terrance Levise Turner, MBA***

Gain 20/20 Vision For The New Decade!
2022 – 365 Day Journal
Document Your Journey!

Living Proverb #1970b: *"Life is full of opportunities to show that you are a champion. Every time you take on the challenge, you will gain a crown."*

~~**Pastor Terrance Levise Turner, MBA**

Gain 20/20 Vision For The New Decade!
2022 – 365 Day Journal
Document Your Journey!

Living Proverb #1971: *"Good things come to those who stay awake!"*

~~Pastor Terrance Levise Turner, MBA

Gain 20/20 Vision For The New Decade!
2022 – 365 Day Journal
Document Your Journey!

Living Proverb #1972: *"Anytime a person is doing too much talking, pay close attention not to pay too much attention."*

~~Pastor Terrance Levise Turner, MBA

Gain 20/20 Vision For The New Decade!
2022 – 365 Day Journal
Document Your Journey!

Living Proverb #1974: *"No complaints. Just action!"*
~~Pastor Terrance Levise Turner, MBA

Gain 20/20 Vision For The New Decade!
2022 – 365 Day Journal
Document Your Journey!

Living Proverb #1975: *"The childish complain and remain. The mature respond and go beyond."*

~~**Pastor Terrance Levise Turner, MBA**

Gain 20/20 Vision For The New Decade!
2022 – 365 Day Journal
Document Your Journey!

Living Proverb #1977: *"Regarding timing, it's always good to know when to say when."*

~~Pastor Terrance Levise Turner, MBA

Gain 20/20 Vision For The New Decade!
2022 – 365 Day Journal
Document Your Journey!

Living Proverb #1978: *"People's behavior in your past informs you of their merits to be a part of your future."*

~~**Pastor Terrance Levise Turner, MBA**

Gain 20/20 Vision For The New Decade!
2022 – 365 Day Journal
Document Your Journey!

Living Proverb #1979: *"Regarding destiny, when God gives you an opportunity to escape the land of mediocrity, never look back, because looking back could be deadly to your dreams."*

~~**Pastor Terrance Levise Turner, MBA**

Gain 20/20 Vision For The New Decade!
2022 – 365 Day Journal
Document Your Journey!

Living Proverb #1984: *"No one can stop anyone who takes the time to transform his or her mind. You can't stop an acorn from becoming an oak tree if it's transformed."*

~~**Pastor Terrance Levise Turner, MBA**

Gain 20/20 Vision For The New Decade!
2022 – 365 Day Journal
Document Your Journey!

Living Proverb #1985: *"God's eyes are "running to and fro" throughout the earth looking for someone to bless. Give Him something to bless by being fruitful, creative, and productive."*
~~**Pastor Terrance Levise Turner, MBA**

Gain 20/20 Vision For The New Decade!
2022 – 365 Day Journal
Document Your Journey!

Living Proverb #1986: *"Let excellence be the signature of your work today. Show people who you are by what you do and the attitude you do it in."*

~~**Pastor Terrance Levise Turner, MBA**

Gain 20/20 Vision For The New Decade!
2022 – 365 Day Journal
Document Your Journey!

Living Proverb #1987: *"Our differences in tastes, inclinations, and passions regarding life and career choice are a testament of the Creator's creativity and of His special consideration of us."*
~~**Pastor Terrance Levise Turner, MBA**

Gain 20/20 Vision For The New Decade!
2022 – 365 Day Journal
Document Your Journey!

Living Proverb #1989: *"Your Christianity should change your personality."*

~~**Pastor Terrance Levise Turner, MBA**

Gain 20/20 Vision For The New Decade!
2022 – 365 Day Journal
Document Your Journey!

Living Proverb #1992: *"Regarding opposition, does the elephant feel the kicking of the ant? Do not be moved by your adversaries. Just keep on marching forward!"*

*~~***Pastor Terrance Levise Turner, MBA***

Gain 20/20 Vision For The New Decade!
2022 – 365 Day Journal
Document Your Journey!

Living Proverb #1993: *"Regarding management, do not be overtaken with anger. Rather, point out the problems, and, then be instructive. Solve by getting involved."*

*~~***Pastor Terrance Levise Turner, MBA***

Gain 20/20 Vision For The New Decade!
2022 – 365 Day Journal
Document Your Journey!

Living Proverb #1994: *"No matter what life tries to put on you, don't let it take what God gave you."*

~~Pastor Terrance Levise Turner, MBA

Gain 20/20 Vision For The New Decade!
2022 – 365 Day Journal
Document Your Journey!

Living Proverb #1996: *"Even those who look for perfection are not perfect."*

~~**Pastor Terrance Levise Turner, MBA**

Gain 20/20 Vision For The New Decade!
2022 – 365 Day Journal
Document Your Journey!

Living Proverb #2001: *"Finance is the discipline of the purveyors of the future."*

~~Pastor Terrance Levise Turner, MBA

Gain 20/20 Vision For The New Decade!
2022 – 365 Day Journal
Document Your Journey!

Living Proverb #2008: *"There's one thing about life, people who've never made a mistake have never made an improvement."*
~~**Pastor Terrance Levise Turner, MBA**

Gain 20/20 Vision For The New Decade!
2022 – 365 Day Journal
Document Your Journey!

Living Proverb #2010: *"Success can be an event, but wealth is a state of being from which you can make continual withdrawals."*
~~**Pastor Terrance Levise Turner, MBA**

Gain 20/20 Vision For The New Decade!
2022 – 365 Day Journal
Document Your Journey!

Living Proverb #2012: *"There are no minor transactions in life. Everything requires thought and prayer."*

~~Pastor Terrance Levise Turner, MBA

Gain 20/20 Vision For The New Decade!
2022 – 365 Day Journal
Document Your Journey!

Living Proverb #2013: *"It may not always be like clockwork when you respond, but always respond responsibly."*

~~Pastor Terrance Levise Turner, MBA

Gain 20/20 Vision For The New Decade!
2022 – 365 Day Journal
Document Your Journey!

Living Proverb #2014: *"If you believe that it's worth it, then, you will make it happen! And, thus, you will make it happen!"*

~~**Pastor Terrance Levise Turner, MBA**

Gain 20/20 Vision For The New Decade!
2022 – 365 Day Journal
Document Your Journey!

Living Proverb #2016: *"Regarding challenges, believe for the best. Yet, prepare for the worst. Either way, God is faithful!"*
~~**Pastor Terrance Levise Turner, MBA**

Gain 20/20 Vision For The New Decade!
2022 – 365 Day Journal
Document Your Journey!

Living Proverb #2018: *"The best thing that you can do for your family and other people is to keep on praying for them. Keep living a righteous life so that you can get a prayer through."*

*~~***Pastor Terrance Levise Turner, MBA***

Gain 20/20 Vision For The New Decade!
2022 – 365 Day Journal
Document Your Journey!

Living Proverb #2019: *"When life gets down to the "nitty-gritty," don't let the grits change you. Rather, you should change the grits. You are salt of the earth."*

~~**Pastor Terrance Levise Turner, MBA**

Gain 20/20 Vision For The New Decade!
2022 – 365 Day Journal
Document Your Journey!

Living Proverb #2020: *"The Word of God is like seeds of light sown into an ocean of darkness. People cling onto that light like clinging onto a life raft during the storms and floods of life."*

*~~***Pastor Terrance Levise Turner, MBA***

Gain 20/20 Vision For The New Decade!
2022 – 365 Day Journal
Document Your Journey!

Living Proverb #2021: *"Being able to see beyond where you are empowers you to go to where you want to be."*

~~Pastor Terrance Levise Turner, MBA

Gain 20/20 Vision For The New Decade!
2022 – 365 Day Journal
Document Your Journey!

Living Proverb #2023: *"Regarding business ventures, have the courage of a naive child, the caution of an experienced adult, and the willingness to learn. Then, make the safest decision."*

*~~***Pastor Terrance Levise Turner, MBA***

Gain 20/20 Vision For The New Decade!
2022 – 365 Day Journal
Document Your Journey!

Living Proverb #2025: *"What you don't know, you can learn. What you don't have, you can earn. Make no room for excuses."*
~~Pastor Terrance Levise Turner, MBA

Gain 20/20 Vision For The New Decade!
2022 – 365 Day Journal
Document Your Journey!

Living Proverb #2026: *"Here is a mystery of faith: stretch out farther than you can comfortably see, and God will take you further than where you may have at first gone."*

~~**Pastor Terrance Levise Turner, MBA**

Gain 20/20 Vision For The New Decade!
2022 – 365 Day Journal
Document Your Journey!

Living Proverb #2027: *"Sometimes God will stretch you beyond your comfort zone in order to alert you to how far you have already grown."*

~~Pastor Terrance Levise Turner, MBA

Gain 20/20 Vision For The New Decade!
2022 – 365 Day Journal
Document Your Journey!

Living Proverb #2028: *"Take advantage of every advantage with thanksgiving."*

~~**Pastor Terrance Levise Turner, MBA**

Gain 20/20 Vision For The New Decade!
2022 – 365 Day Journal
Document Your Journey!

Living Proverb #2031: *"The Bible is not philosophy. The Bible is truth. Obeying it or not obeying it is a matter of life or death."*
~~Pastor Terrance Levise Turner, MBA

Gain 20/20 Vision For The New Decade!
2022 – 365 Day Journal
Document Your Journey!

Living Proverb #2033: *"Don't focus on your problems. Focus on your blessings. If you focus on your blessings, your blessings will multiply."*

~~**Pastor Terrance Levise Turner, MBA**

Gain 20/20 Vision For The New Decade!
2022 – 365 Day Journal
Document Your Journey!

Living Proverb #2038: *"Wealth is a matter of perspective. Elisha, the prophet, didn't give the widow with the "pot of oil" one thin dime. He only changed her paradigm to a wealth mentality."*

~~Pastor Terrance Levise Turner, MBA

Gain 20/20 Vision For The New Decade!
2022 – 365 Day Journal
Document Your Journey!

Living Proverb #2039: *"Everyday is not going to be a knockout. What matters most is that you fought the full twelve rounds. You are still the champion, even if you won by a TKO."*

~~**Pastor Terrance Levise Turner, MBA**

Gain 20/20 Vision For The New Decade!
2022 – 365 Day Journal
Document Your Journey!

Living Proverb #2040: *"Regarding business, if you know what you're doing, then, you can compete. If you don't know what you're doing, then, you can learn. Either way, you're a contender."*

~~**Pastor Terrance Levise Turner, MBA**

Gain 20/20 Vision For The New Decade!
2022 – 365 Day Journal
Document Your Journey!

Living Proverb #2041: *"Regarding succeeding, if at first you seem uncertain, then, continue to take steps, gaining knowledge along the way, and you'll become more and more certain as you go."*

~~**Pastor Terrance Levise Turner, MBA**

Gain 20/20 Vision For The New Decade!
2022 – 365 Day Journal
Document Your Journey!

Living Proverb #2042: *"Life is filled with opportunities. Life is filled with choices. The deciding factor is how you choose to take them."*

~~Pastor Terrance Levise Turner, MBA

Gain 20/20 Vision For The New Decade!
2022 – 365 Day Journal
Document Your Journey!

Living Proverb #2043: *"Some things that stress–out others, fuels others. There are some things that you're just born for! Your wealth is in your anointing!"*

*~~***Pastor Terrance Levise Turner, MBA**

Gain 20/20 Vision For The New Decade!
2022 – 365 Day Journal
Document Your Journey!

Living Proverb #2044: *"Life is like "Shawshank Redemption." If you keep chipping at the wall with the sharp instruments of your mind and efforts, you will eventually break through to freedom!"*

~~Pastor Terrance Levise Turner, MBA

Gain 20/20 Vision For The New Decade!
2022 – 365 Day Journal
Document Your Journey!

Living Proverb #2045: *"Always treat people with courtesy, kindness, and consideration. Sometimes people could be hanging on by a thread. You could be that thread."*

~~**Pastor Terrance Levise Turner, MBA**

Gain 20/20 Vision For The New Decade!
2022 – 365 Day Journal
Document Your Journey!

Living Proverb #2046: *"If you get the fire going by practicing the spark of genius God has given you, then, He will give you an opportunity to flare into a raging success!"*

~~**Pastor Terrance Levise Turner, MBA**

Gain 20/20 Vision For The New Decade!
2022 – 365 Day Journal
Document Your Journey!

Living Proverb #2047: *"If you would truly release the energy of your whole personality, then, you could empower the entire world!"*
~~**Pastor Terrance Levise Turner, MBA**

Gain 20/20 Vision For The New Decade!
2022 – 365 Day Journal
Document Your Journey!

Living Proverb #2048b: *"The vision will determine the success. If you can detect the size of the vision, you will determine the possibility for success. How clear and how much do you see?"*

*~~***Pastor Terrance Levise Turner, MBA***

Gain 20/20 Vision For The New Decade!
2022 – 365 Day Journal
Document Your Journey!

Living Proverb #2050: *"Confess wealth and prosperity with your mouth. Believe it in your heart. Then, take action on what you say. You will be saved from poverty. It will be true in your life"*

~~Pastor Terrance Levise Turner, MBA

Gain 20/20 Vision For The New Decade!
2022 – 365 Day Journal
Document Your Journey!

Living Proverb #2051: *"Regarding success, pray fervently, plan carefully, and work diligently. Success is obtainable. It is the will of God for you."*

*~~***Pastor Terrance Levise Turner, MBA***

Gain 20/20 Vision For The New Decade!
2022 – 365 Day Journal
Document Your Journey!

Living Proverb #2052: *"Mental liberation leads to emotional liberation. If the Son sets you free from fear, you shall be free indeed."*

~~**Pastor Terrance Levise Turner, MBA**

Gain 20/20 Vision For The New Decade!
2022 – 365 Day Journal
Document Your Journey!

Living Proverb #2053: *"During times of change is a good time to change. When life is making natural or unusual shifts is a good time to evaluate your life to see where you need to change."*

~~Pastor Terrance Levise Turner, MBA

Gain 20/20 Vision For The New Decade!
2022 – 365 Day Journal
Document Your Journey!

Living Proverb #2054: *"It's the small things that make the difference between a winner and a loser. Discipline yourself and you will then be able to cross the finish line as an undeniable victor!"*

~~**Pastor Terrance Levise Turner, MBA**

Gain 20/20 Vision For The New Decade!
2022 – 365 Day Journal
Document Your Journey!

Living Proverb #2055: *"When life says something to you it pays to listen. Whether it's the death of a friend or loved one, an unusual symptom, cut-backs in the economy, etc., it pays to listen."*
~~**Pastor Terrance Levise Turner, MBA**

Gain 20/20 Vision For The New Decade!
2022 – 365 Day Journal
Document Your Journey!

Living Proverb #2056: *"Regarding success and progress, you don't necessarily have to forget where you came from, but you definitely have to leave."*

~~**Pastor Terrance Levise Turner, MBA**

Gain 20/20 Vision For The New Decade!
2022 – 365 Day Journal
Document Your Journey!

Living Proverb #2057: "*Regarding relationships, we must intentionally endeavor to keep the unity of the spirit, in the bond of peace. Peace binds people together. Strife separates.*"

~~**Pastor Terrance Levise Turner, MBA**

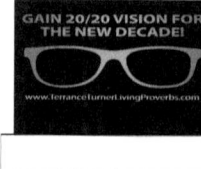

Gain 20/20 Vision For The New Decade!
2022 – 365 Day Journal
Document Your Journey!

Living Proverb #2058: *"Regarding helping people with problems, you may help them out of a fix, but you can't fix their problem. They have to do something long-term to fix their own problems."*

~~**Pastor Terrance Levise Turner, MBA**

Gain 20/20 Vision For The New Decade!
2022 – 365 Day Journal
Document Your Journey!

Living Proverb #2059: *"If you're still alive, and your dream is still alive, then, you can still achieve your dream."*
~~**Pastor Terrance Levise Turner, MBA**

Gain 20/20 Vision For The New Decade!
2022 – 365 Day Journal
Document Your Journey!

Living Proverb #2061: *"Wealth won't come without go!."*
~~**Pastor Terrance Levise Turner, MBA**

Gain 20/20 Vision For The New Decade!
2022 – 365 Day Journal
Document Your Journey!

Living Proverb #2063: *"A faithful man is not a perfect man. He's just a man faithful to continue striving to be the best that he can be in every situation. He will be faithful to God's principles."*
~~**Pastor Terrance Levise Turner, MBA**

Gain 20/20 Vision For The New Decade!
2022 – 365 Day Journal
Document Your Journey!

Living Proverb #2066: *"Regarding creativity, a lot of times the process can be messy, but when it's finished, it can be beautiful!"*
~~**Pastor Terrance Levise Turner, MBA**

Gain 20/20 Vision For The New Decade!
2022 – 365 Day Journal
Document Your Journey!

Living Proverb #2067: *"If the saints will focus again on saving souls, a whole lot of our problems will just work themselves out."*
~~Pastor Terrance Levise Turner, MBA

Gain 20/20 Vision For The New Decade!
2022 – 365 Day Journal
Document Your Journey!

Living Proverb #2068: *"Regarding problems, don't complain about the fire of life. If you're the real deal, then, you will shine brighter. The refiners fire makes the pure gold shine brighter."*

*~~***Pastor Terrance Levise Turner, MBA***

Gain 20/20 Vision For The New Decade!
2022 – 365 Day Journal
Document Your Journey!

Living Proverb #2069: *"To be successful spiritually or financially then, you have to leave your old crowd. If you want to be saved or prosperous, then, you've got to leave the old crowd."*

*~~***Pastor Terrance Levise Turner, MBA***

Gain 20/20 Vision For The New Decade!
2022 – 365 Day Journal
Document Your Journey!

Living Proverb #2076: *"Just like Oprah Winfrey had the aspiration and ambition to strive pass her initial talent to own her OWN network, you too should strive for ownership in your own life."*
~~**Pastor Terrance Levise Turner, MBA**

Gain 20/20 Vision For The New Decade!
2022 – 365 Day Journal
Document Your Journey!

Living Proverb #2078: *"Regarding humility, you should be as bold as you need to be to do what God called you to do. Make yourself of no reputation, but let your obedience speak for you."*

*~~***Pastor Terrance Levise Turner, MBA**

Gain 20/20 Vision For The New Decade!
2022 – 365 Day Journal
Document Your Journey!

Living Proverb #2080: *"Embrace your youth. Make the most of it. Be bold. Be strong. Be courageous. Then, when it's time, thank God for a head of white hair. It's a badge of honor you've grown into."*
~~**Pastor Terrance Levise Turner, MBA**

Gain 20/20 Vision For The New Decade!
2022 – 365 Day Journal
Document Your Journey!

Living Proverb #2082: *"There's nothing wrong with "tooting your own horn" if you know you are a golden trumpet."*
~~Pastor Terrance Levise Turner, MBA

Gain 20/20 Vision For The New Decade!
2022 – 365 Day Journal
Document Your Journey!

Living Proverb #2084: *"Conversations are like driving through a drive-through. Always assume that at least 50% of the requested content might have been left out! Always check your bag."*

*~~***Pastor Terrance Levise Turner, MBA***

Gain 20/20 Vision For The New Decade!
2022 – 365 Day Journal
Document Your Journey!

Living Proverb #2085: *"If you'll spend the time that you spend talking about the problem to pray about the problem, then, you'll solve the problem."*

~~**Pastor Terrance Levise Turner, MBA**

Gain 20/20 Vision For The New Decade!
2022 – 365 Day Journal
Document Your Journey!

Living Proverb #2086: *"Regarding happiness, focus on what God has already done, and put your faith in what He's capable of doing. You'll be less stressed and happier."*

*~~***Pastor Terrance Levise Turner, MBA**

Gain 20/20 Vision For The New Decade!
2022 – 365 Day Journal
Document Your Journey!

Living Proverb #2087: *"Problem prevention is the key to solving problems."*

~~Pastor Terrance Levise Turner, MBA

Gain 20/20 Vision For The New Decade!
2022 – 365 Day Journal
Document Your Journey!

Living Proverb #2090: *"Concerning faith, you don't need a co-signer regarding your faith. You must hear from God for yourself. You must get your assignment. You must know your own heart."*

*~~***Pastor Terrance Levise Turner, MBA***

Gain 20/20 Vision For The New Decade!
2022 – 365 Day Journal
Document Your Journey!

Living Proverb #2093: *"When you spendeth, then, money goeth. When you soweth, then, money cometh. But, you still have to be wise in your money management."*

~~**Pastor Terrance Levise Turner, MBA**

Gain 20/20 Vision For The New Decade!
2022 – 365 Day Journal
Document Your Journey!

Living Proverb #2094: *"Regarding influence, either you will be shaped or you will be a shaper. In most cases, it will be both. There is no neutral ground."*

~~**Pastor Terrance Levise Turner, MBA**

Gain 20/20 Vision For The New Decade!
2022 – 365 Day Journal
Document Your Journey!

Living Proverb #2096: *"Regarding budgeting, savings, investing, exercising, family time, church attendance, etc., the key to lasting success is a regular schedule, rather than a random schedule."*
~~**Pastor Terrance Levise Turner, MBA**

Gain 20/20 Vision For The New Decade!
2022 – 365 Day Journal
Document Your Journey!

Living Proverb #2097: *"Regarding other people's business, assumption usually reveals ignorance. Tend to your own business, because that's the only place that you are qualified to be an expert."*
~~**Pastor Terrance Levise Turner, MBA**

Gain 20/20 Vision For The New Decade!
2022 – 365 Day Journal
Document Your Journey!

Living Proverb #2098: *"The instructions of God bring structure to our lives. If we build our lives upon the instructions of the Bible, our lives will be more stable."*

~~Pastor Terrance Levise Turner, MBA

Gain 20/20 Vision For The New Decade!
2022 – 365 Day Journal
Document Your Journey!

Living Proverb #2099: *"Regarding success and progress, the words 'I agree' are two of the most powerful words in regard to cooperation with others and with God. 'I agree.'"*

~~**Pastor Terrance Levise Turner, MBA**

Gain 20/20 Vision For The New Decade!
2022 – 365 Day Journal
Document Your Journey!

Living Proverb #2100: *"The Word of God will blow your natural mind! It will get you saved. It will get you healed. It will get you delivered. So, be expectant! The Word will transform your life."'*

*~~***Pastor Terrance Levise Turner, MBA***

Gain 20/20 Vision For The New Decade!
2022 – 365 Day Journal
Document Your Journey!

Living Proverb #2101: *"Just because others don't hear your prayers, doesn't mean God doesn't. The effectual, fervent prayers of a righteous person avails much.'"*

~~**Pastor Terrance Levise Turner, MBA**

Gain 20/20 Vision For The New Decade!
2022 – 365 Day Journal
Document Your Journey!

Living Proverb #2102: *"One thing about God is that He doesn't count people out for lack of perfection. But, He does measure intent."*

~~**Pastor Terrance Levise Turner, MBA**

Gain 20/20 Vision For The New Decade!
2022 – 365 Day Journal
Document Your Journey!

Living Proverb #2104: *"Purpose is the why. Focus helps you see the how. Passion fuels the vision."*

*~~***Pastor Terrance Levise Turner, MBA***

Gain 20/20 Vision For The New Decade!
2022 – 365 Day Journal
Document Your Journey!

Living Proverb #2105: *"The Words of God are like living stones cast upon the sea of life. No matter how stormy your life, keep stepping out on His Words. You will make it safely to the other side."*
~~**Pastor Terrance Levise Turner, MBA**

Gain 20/20 Vision For The New Decade!
2022 – 365 Day Journal
Document Your Journey!

Living Proverb #2106: *"One of the best investments that you can make into your future is motivation!"*

~~**Pastor Terrance Levise Turner, MBA**

Gain 20/20 Vision For The New Decade!
2022 – 365 Day Journal
Document Your Journey!

Living Proverb #2107: *"He is a friend who forces you to hunt for your own food, catch your own fish, and harvest your own field. He is a foe who feeds you with welfare without labor."*

*~~***Pastor Terrance Levise Turner, MBA***

Gain 20/20 Vision For The New Decade!
2022 – 365 Day Journal
Document Your Journey!

Living Proverb #2111: *"People who practice high values have greater practical value. People who practice low or no values have lesser practical value."*

~~**Pastor Terrance Levise Turner, MBA**

Gain 20/20 Vision For The New Decade!
2022 – 365 Day Journal
Document Your Journey!

Living Proverb #2112: *"Regarding success, it takes a lot to start it up. It takes a lot to build it up. And, if you want to keep it up, it takes a lot to keep it up!"*

~~**Pastor Terrance Levise Turner, MBA**

Gain 20/20 Vision For The New Decade!
2022 – 365 Day Journal
Document Your Journey!

Living Proverb #2114: *"Circumspection and discretion are keys to promotion for you to learn as early as possible. They are critical to your successful future"*

~~**Pastor Terrance Levise Turner, MBA**

Gain 20/20 Vision For The New Decade!
2022 – 365 Day Journal
Document Your Journey!

Living Proverb #2115: *"When you're someone who gives outstanding service, then, you're going straight to the top! Because, a positive attitude will take you straight to the top!"*
~~**Pastor Terrance Levise Turner, MBA**

Gain 20/20 Vision For The New Decade!
2022 – 365 Day Journal
Document Your Journey!

Living Proverb #2116: *"Leadership can be inspiring, uplifting, and affirming. Inspiring leadership builds people up and causes them to grow, increase, and be their very best!"*

~~**Pastor Terrance Levise Turner, MBA**

Gain 20/20 Vision For The New Decade!
2022 – 365 Day Journal
Document Your Journey!

Living Proverb #2117a: *"If you're in management, you're not being paid the big money to handle the routine parts of your job. Rather, you're being paid to solve the problems!"*

~~**Pastor Terrance Levise Turner, MBA**

Gain 20/20 Vision For The New Decade!
2022 – 365 Day Journal
Document Your Journey!

Living Proverb #2117b: *"Minimum wage is the pay for minimum problems. Maximum wages require maximum wisdom!"*

~~**Pastor Terrance Levise Turner, MBA**

Gain 20/20 Vision For The New Decade!
2022 – 365 Day Journal
Document Your Journey!

Living Proverb #2118: *"Skill, education, and determination can change your situation and station in life. Get it, and use it!"*
~~Pastor Terrance Levise Turner, MBA

Gain 20/20 Vision For The New Decade!
2022 – 365 Day Journal
Document Your Journey!

Living Proverb #2119: *"Regarding trouble, it's better to ignore insignificant trouble that doesn't belong to you."*

~~**Pastor Terrance Levise Turner, MBA**

Gain 20/20 Vision For The New Decade!
2022 – 365 Day Journal
Document Your Journey!

Living Proverb #2123: *"Life is a given. What you make of it is up to you."*

~~Pastor Terrance Levise Turner, MBA

Gain 20/20 Vision For The New Decade!
2022 – 365 Day Journal
Document Your Journey!

Living Proverb #2123: *"Success takes time, but if you take the time, then, you will succeed."*

*~~***Pastor Terrance Levise Turner, MBA***

Gain 20/20 Vision For The New Decade!
2022 – 365 Day Journal
Document Your Journey!

Living Proverb #2125: *"Refine your gifts and talents. Turn them into skills. Get your education. Put forth effort, and you will guarantee a profitable result."*

*~~***Pastor Terrance Levise Turner, MBA**

Gain 20/20 Vision For The New Decade!
2022 – 365 Day Journal
Document Your Journey!

Living Proverb #2127: *"Regarding life and work, giving yourself a break will keep you from breaking."*

~~**Pastor Terrance Levise Turner, MBA**

Gain 20/20 Vision For The New Decade!
2022 – 365 Day Journal
Document Your Journey!

Living Proverb #2128: *"Regarding breakfast, a good start will keep you going strong."*

~~Pastor Terrance Levise Turner, MBA

Gain 20/20 Vision For The New Decade!
2022 – 365 Day Journal
Document Your Journey!

Living Proverb #2129: *"Without ambition there's no ignition. Faith is the substance of things hoped for!"*
~~**Pastor Terrance Levise Turner, MBA**

Gain 20/20 Vision For The New Decade!
2022 – 365 Day Journal
Document Your Journey!

Living Proverb #2130: *"Words are valuable. So, make your words count for something that will last for eternity."*

~~Pastor Terrance Levise Turner, MBA

Gain 20/20 Vision For The New Decade!
2022 – 365 Day Journal
Document Your Journey!

Living Proverb #2131: *"In your patience, you maintain possession of your own soul. You will not be flailed about in life by circumstances, people's personalities, or events."*

~~**Pastor Terrance Levise Turner, MBA**

Gain 20/20 Vision For The New Decade!
2022 – 365 Day Journal
Document Your Journey!

Living Proverb #2132: *"Wealth is about creating value. Wealth is not just about making money. Money can be here today and gone tomorrow. Yet, value can make money all day long."*

~~**Pastor Terrance Levise Turner, MBA**

Gain 20/20 Vision For The New Decade!
2022 – 365 Day Journal
Document Your Journey!

Living Proverb #2137: *"Practice loving yourself. Others will love you like you love you."*

~~**Pastor Terrance Levise Turner, MBA**

Gain 20/20 Vision For The New Decade!
2022 – 365 Day Journal
Document Your Journey!

Living Proverb #2140: *"Pray anyway. Your problems may seem like a small thing in light of the big picture. But, remember, the big picture is made up of small things. Pray anyway."*

~~**Pastor Terrance Levise Turner, MBA**

Gain 20/20 Vision For The New Decade!
2022 – 365 Day Journal
Document Your Journey!

Living Proverb #2141: *"An essential part of doing is knowing. Once you know what to do, then, you can do it. Make knowing a priority. An essential part of doing is knowing."*

~~**Pastor Terrance Levise Turner, MBA**

Gain 20/20 Vision For The New Decade!
2022 – 365 Day Journal
Document Your Journey!

Living Proverb #2143: *"God isn't as interested in you living by miracles, as He is in you living by His method. He wants you to learn to live by His method, so that you can teach your children."*

~~Pastor Terrance Levise Turner, MBA

Gain 20/20 Vision For The New Decade!
2022 – 365 Day Journal
Document Your Journey!

Living Proverb #2144: *"Facts are relative. Truth is timeless. Build your life on the truth and you will be stable. You will endure the shifting facts of time."*

~~**Pastor Terrance Levise Turner, MBA**

Gain 20/20 Vision For The New Decade!
2022 – 365 Day Journal
Document Your Journey!

Living Proverb #2145: *"Wages come from doing what you've got to do. Riches come from doing what you get to do."*
~~Pastor Terrance Levise Turner, MBA

Gain 20/20 Vision For The New Decade!
2022 – 365 Day Journal
Document Your Journey!

Living Proverb #2146: *"There's nothing wrong with not knowing, not having experience, or not being sure as long as you keep learning, growing, and increasing in pursuit of knowledge."*

*~~***Pastor Terrance Levise Turner, MBA***

Gain 20/20 Vision For The New Decade!
2022 – 365 Day Journal
Document Your Journey!

Living Proverb #2147: *"Success is a process. Profit takes time. However, if you don't go through the process, you'll never receive the profit."*

~~**Pastor Terrance Levise Turner, MBA**

Gain 20/20 Vision For The New Decade!
2022 – 365 Day Journal
Document Your Journey!

Living Proverb #2149: *"You only have one life to live. Therefore, squeeze all of the juice that you can out of that lemon, and make lemonade! Then, you can refresh the lives of others along the way."*

~~**Pastor Terrance Levise Turner, MBA**

Gain 20/20 Vision For The New Decade!
2022 – 365 Day Journal
Document Your Journey!

Living Proverb #2150: *"You have to live your life like an economist. Don't be so moved by the ups and downs. Rather, watch the trends."*

~~**Pastor Terrance Levise Turner, MBA**

Gain 20/20 Vision For The New Decade!
2022 – 365 Day Journal
Document Your Journey!

Living Proverb #2151: *"As you mature in life, you should become more sober without becoming sour."*

~~**Pastor Terrance Levise Turner, MBA**

Gain 20/20 Vision For The New Decade!
2022 – 365 Day Journal
Document Your Journey!

Living Proverb #2152: *"Why spend all of your time and energy fighting to be a slave? When you can use that same time and energy to fight to be free. Start that business. You can succeed."*

~~**Pastor Terrance Levise Turner, MBA**

Gain 20/20 Vision For The New Decade!
2022 – 365 Day Journal
Document Your Journey!

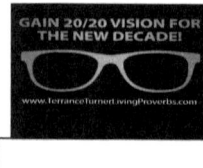

Living Proverb #2153: *"It's good to get outside consultation and help. However, always keep the main thing the main thing, and keep your core strong. You are your source of wealth."*

~~**Pastor Terrance Levise Turner, MBA**

Gain 20/20 Vision For The New Decade!
2022 – 365 Day Journal
Document Your Journey!

Living Proverb #2154: *"Don't be afraid. The same God that has been taking care of you all of these years is the same God that will continue to shelter you. Don't be afraid."*

~~**Pastor Terrance Levise Turner, MBA**

Gain 20/20 Vision For The New Decade!
2022 – 365 Day Journal
Document Your Journey!

Living Proverb #2155: *"Regarding hard work, always take time to rest. Every flow needs to ebb."*

~~**Pastor Terrance Levise Turner, MBA**

Gain 20/20 Vision For The New Decade!
2022 – 365 Day Journal
Document Your Journey!

Living Proverb #2156: *"Regarding reputation, you have to prove yourself until you prove yourself. You prove yourself to others through your results."*

~~**Pastor Terrance Levise Turner, MBA**

Gain 20/20 Vision For The New Decade!
2022 – 365 Day Journal
Document Your Journey!

Living Proverb #2157: *"Use what God gave you to do what God made you to do to get what God has for you."*

~~**Pastor Terrance Levise Turner, MBA**

Gain 20/20 Vision For The New Decade!
2022 – 365 Day Journal
Document Your Journey!

Living Proverb #2159: *"Regarding destiny, if you've done anything else, then, you can do everything else that's required for you to obtain your destiny!"*

~~**Pastor Terrance Levise Turner, MBA**

Gain 20/20 Vision For The New Decade!
2022 – 365 Day Journal
Document Your Journey!

Living Proverb #2163: *"Never neglect prayer and Bible study to give more time to work. One hour of dedicated prayer and Bible study will empower you for a full 12 hours of work. Always pray."*

*~~***Pastor Terrance Levise Turner, MBA***

Gain 20/20 Vision For The New Decade!
2022 – 365 Day Journal
Document Your Journey!

Living Proverb #2164: *"Always take time to pray. Sacrifice on the front end will prevent losses on the back end. Always acknowledge the Lord."*

~~Pastor Terrance Levise Turner, MBA

Gain 20/20 Vision For The New Decade!
2022 – 365 Day Journal
Document Your Journey!

Living Proverb #2165: *"When consulting wise people, sometimes you have to look past the presentation in order to access the content."*

*~~***Pastor Terrance Levise Turner, MBA***

Gain 20/20 Vision For The New Decade!
2022 – 365 Day Journal
Document Your Journey!

Living Proverb #2166: "*Regarding how to become rich, the person who walks with wise people shall become wise. The person who walks with rich people shall become rich.*"

~~**Pastor Terrance Levise Turner, MBA**

Gain 20/20 Vision For The New Decade!
2022 – 365 Day Journal
Document Your Journey!

Living Proverb #2168: *"Conversation with a hundred-thousandnaire is different than a millionaire or billionaire. If you want to be a millionaire, then, listen to a millionaire or billionaire."*

*~~***Pastor Terrance Levise Turner, MBA***

Gain 20/20 Vision For The New Decade!
2022 – 365 Day Journal
Document Your Journey!

Living Proverb #2169: *"Receiving information from a billionaire increases the possibility of you becoming at least a millionaire."*
~~Pastor Terrance Levise Turner, MBA

Gain 20/20 Vision For The New Decade!
2022 – 365 Day Journal
Document Your Journey!

Living Proverb #2173: *"Faith is taking action on what you hope for. Action is the evidence that you believe what you do not see. Action gives substance to the dream you talk about."*

*~~***Pastor Terrance Levise Turner, MBA**

Gain 20/20 Vision For The New Decade!
2022 – 365 Day Journal
Document Your Journey!

Living Proverb #2174: *"You should seek the blessing God promises to every person who worships and reverences Him. He desires you to profit from your labor and to be happy in life."*

*~~***Pastor Terrance Levise Turner, MBA***

Gain 20/20 Vision For The New Decade!
2022 – 365 Day Journal
Document Your Journey!

Living Proverb #2183: *"Regarding the journey toward your destiny, learn to enjoy the blessings along the way to your destination. You will better appreciate it when you have arrived."*

~~**Pastor Terrance Levise Turner, MBA**

Gain 20/20 Vision For The New Decade!
2022 – 365 Day Journal
Document Your Journey!

Gain 20/20 Vision For The New Decade!
2022 – 365 Day Journal
Document Your Journey!